1

To Mom Thank you 1

To my amazing wife, Brenda Thank you for standing beside (and usually slightly I front of) me.

To Debbie Willis Thank you for inspiring me. You are the reason I love books.

To Mrs. Graham Thank you for your time. It's amazing the difference a substitute teacher can make!

Treasure?

The old man's rocking chair squeaked in a perfect rhythm against his wooden porch. Each squall came in exactly the same amount of time as the last one. Staring at the giant bluffs of the Superstition Mountains in front of him, the squeaking stopped when his grandson broke the quiet symphony with a snapping bite of his apple. As the juice poured out of his mouth, he asked his Grandpa, with overly full cheeks, "Grandpa, you've spent a lifetime out in those mountains looking for the Lost Dutchman's Gold Mine. Do you think you'll ever find it?"

The old man's eyes reflected decades of trips into the massive, wild, unforgiving wilderness that lay in front of them. Countless trips into the desert played out in his old faded eyes, blocking his view of the steep bluffs that he knew by heart. He thought about all he learned looking for a mine that had always eluded him. He rocked his squeaky chair back one more time. Smiling, he revealed the few teeth he had left and said, "I sure hope not."

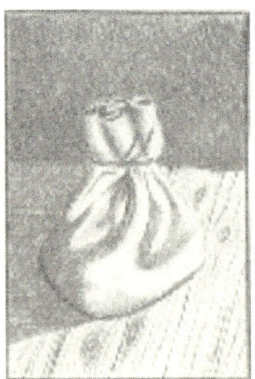

The Search

The Story of a Lost Fortune and a Truth About it's Finding.

Table of Contents

Chapter 1...A fall

Chapter 2...The don

Chapter 3...A grave

Chapter 4...The mine

Chapter 5...A tree

Chapter 6...The stranger

Chapter 7...A stack of money

Chapter 8...The debt

Chapter 9...A growing storm

Chapter 10.......................................The uninvited

Chapter 11.......................................A rock

Chapter 12.......................................The last trip

Chapter 13.......................................A truth

Chapter 14.......................................The end

Chapter 15.......................................A beginning

No idea is so outlandish that it should not be considered with a searching, but at the same time, a steady eye.

-Winston Churchill-

Chapter 1

A Fall

-A thing is not necessarily true because a man dies for it- **Oscar Wilde**

"DO NOT LET GO!" The words exploded out of Paul's mouth in the same instant that he realized he was the one holding on. How could this happen? He had spent his entire adult life taking people into this remote area of Arizona. He was too good to have an accident like this on his watch.

Sweat rolled off the tip of his nose as he stared down at a 1500 foot drop below. Different parts of the man he was clutching seemed to dominate his field of view. His mind did not want to accept that he was holding on to a human being. It wasn't like in the movies. The force and weight that hit his arms when he caught the man had definitely injured Paul. Judging by the popping sound each shoulder made he was certain they both were dislocated, but right now he could not feel any pain.

All he felt was fear.

He could hear the dusty gravel grinding under his knees against the rock beneath him. He realized that he was following the man to a shared fate. Paul was holding the green, nylon straps of a backpack in his left hand and a sweaty wrist in his right that was slipping all the time. The wrist and the straps were carrying the joint tearing weight of a man suspended over the edge. All Paul could focus on was the straps and the wrist. He was separating himself from the person seconds away from death, who was laid across the abrupt, jagged downturn of a rock. Not just any rock, but the biggest rock on the top of Tortilla Mountain.

It was so big that it looked like a part of the mountain, and it perched precariously on the edge of the giant mesa. The rock should have had a name like Lookout Point or Castle Rock but, like many places in these mountains, it did not. It was so far removed from anything important that it had gone nameless.

Suddenly a map erupted out of the old green backpack with the wind. It screamed past Paul's face. In a fraction of eternity the worn map opened as it ripped past his eyes. He could make out one landmark and when he saw it, his breath vanished. Of all the locations to present itself to Paul's psyche, this one meant the most. A 1000 foot spire rose dramatically from the desert floor. It looked like a hundred concentric circles so close together that they all touched on the map.

It was Weavers Needle.

Despite the unnerving desperation of the moment, a slice of recent history immediately took over Paul's thinking. And as the scene played out uncontrollably in his mind, Paul let out a groan that, to the onlookers, seemed to be the product of physical exertion. But it was really the audible pain of an opportunity lost. Paul's thoughts landed on a week-old conversation.

"Paul, there is no way I can just erase Weavers Needle off the map." Walt couldn't make himself look his older brother in the eye. Just saying no to him was hard enough. He was nearly a foot shorter than the man who had, by all rights raised him.

"Little brother," Paul put a heavy emphasis on the word little, "it always comes up. It's the first thing people ask me about." The two were verbally jousting across the bed of an old pickup. The rust spots and dings seemed to match the stains and rips of Paul's clothes to a tee. Though Walt had no more money than Paul, his appearance was much cleaner.

"That is why it's a bad idea to take it off." Walt's voice tapered almost to a whisper as he tried to kick a small rock and missed. "Paul, don't you think someone will notice that Weavers Needle, the biggest clue to the mine, is missing?"

"I'm just tired of explaining it. Every trip some city-ot," Paul smiled at the pairing of city and idiot, "either asks what it's named after or tells me how much he already knows about Pauline Weaver." The smile melted away. "Then they ask me what kind of name is Pauline for a man, or was Pauline a woman. It just ruins my whole day."

"You used to be proud to be named after him." Walt looked up into the heavy silence between himself and his much older brother. Grinding teeth broke the silence.

"Well that's the one good thing I got when I turned twelve," the reference caused Walt to look away, "I got a new name." Paul leaned in fast towards Walt, as if he were throwing the words with his mouth.

"Paul I've been thinking," Walt quickly changed the subject, "this con, well, how long does it last?" Walt's foot made contact with the rock this time.

"We don't have many options. As handsome as I am, I can't buy groceries with my looks buddy." Paul's charm erased his anger. He half-smiled and winked at Walt, who did not return the favor. "Walt, look I am doing the best I can to keep us in groceries. I know you don't like being caught up in this. You're a good man. But buddy, one day we will find it. You know that if anyone will, it's me. There's enough gold left in the Lost Dutchman to put an end to all of this." Paul waved his right hand in the air, as if that was where the lie existed.

"The mine is hiring again." Walt pressed himself hard against the truck, bracing for what he knew was coming.

"The mine!" Paul's emotions jumped again, from one extreme to another. "The Peters and Ford mine! You want to trade your soul to those snakes for a few bucks? Did you forget what they took from us?" Both of Paul's hands shot up in the air this time. Then he dropped them behind his head and laced his fingers together, as though he were keeping them from doing something to Walt that he would regret.

"They didn't kill Momma Paul, cancer did." Dust floated in the air around them as if it had been blown off of the subject for the first time in decades.

Paul's hands dropped into fists by his side. He spoke a Clint Eastwood whisper through gritted teeth, saying, "You weren't old enough to understand Walt. You weren't even two on my twelfth birthday. There is no way you can remember Dad telling us Momma would die because we didn't have enough money to save her! You were sitting in a dirty diaper, on a hand-me-down couch, in a house that we rented from that rat-hole company!" The whisper grew into shouting. "Did you know that Raelene's mom had the same cancer that Momma had? She's still alive today! Want to know why Walt? Because Raelene's daddy was a board member. He made sure Dad's checks were as small as possible, Walt! He made money doing nothing while Dad broke his back in that stinking hole in the ground! Do you want the same life Dad had, Walt?" Paul shouted his question.

Walt's quiet reply contrasted the intensity of his brother's rage. "Paul, we can't keep cheating folks. You could end it today, just call it off and give the people their money back. It has already gotten out of control. You want me to erase Weavers Needle right now. We can't just erase everything you don't like." Paul's hands opened from the fists he had been holding.

"Fine, leave Weavers Needle on the map." Paul turned and got in the driver seat of the old truck. The old wreck rocked back and forth from the violent slamming of the door. Paul left, without saying goodbye to Walt. He drove straight to the rental car company. As he got out of his old jalopy, a man met him in the lot, jingling a set of keys. "She's all ready for you Mr. Michaels," the sharply dressed lot attendant sung out. Paul answered in like, changing his whole countenance like the charming, chameleon he was.

"That is why I use you! Best customer service in the valley!" Paul smiled. He stepped into a large, white, four wheel drive van that would comfortably hold the gear and passengers which would both be decimated by the end of the week. He sped off to Sky Harbor Airport to pick up the clients that were anxious for Paul to guide them to their fortune. Paul turned up the hard rock station that was playing on the radio and basked again in his rage. Then, moments before pulling over at the rendezvous, he turned the radio down. As Paul stepped out of the van the fury dropped from his face. He smiled, stuck out his hand and said, "Welcome to the trip of a lifetime!"

The thin green straps of the pack were digging ferociously into Paul's fingers. He had crammed the tips of them all into the heel of his hand but his forefinger and pinky were being pried away by the nylon stretched around them. The slow grind of gravel between the rock and his knees increased as he felt a hand on his back. Suddenly he was knocked to his stomach and closer to death.

One of the clients had tried to help Paul, but in his zeal had only made things worse. Paul was now nothing more than an anchor for the falling man. He had no way to pull against the strain. The hand that knocked him down quickly grabbed the back of his belt which only pulled his jeans down, but did not stop his forward momentum much. Paul screamed "Let go! Get my feet, my feet!"

Suddenly the trail below came into his view as the client grabbed his feet and slowed the fall, causing the pain of his dislocated shoulders to appear. The sweaty wrist was growing harder and harder to hold. Paul tried desperately to focus on the straps and the wrist. But the bend in the trail had been another pivotal point. As the helplessness of Paul's new situation set in, his mind would only consider all of the times when this could have been avoided. The bend in the trail below him was the last of those moments.

"Think I can stand on the point of that rock?" Paul asked, jerking his massive thumb upwards towards the rock on top of Tortilla Mountain.

"No, Paul I don't think you could stand on top of that rock" said the female client, her voice dripping with the new disdain she had acquired for Paul.

"I haven't been on top of this rock, but let's give it a shot."

Paul would sometimes lie, even when the truth sounded better. The truth was that he had been on top of that rock countless times, which would have offered credibility to him as a man and a guide. But the lie made him look silly and created a literal death trap this time.

"You see," which are usually the first words spoken by a liar, cheater, politician or some condescending person of ill-repute when they are about to bend the truth, "these rocks are special. All of these big rocks were used by the Apache Indians as lookout points. They would stand on top and watch for bands of enemy Indians coming to attack them. Sometimes one Indian would spend weeks on top of these rocks."

"Isn't the term Indian derogatory?" the socially aware client asked, her face twisting at the word.

"I guess I've still got a lot of John Wayne in me." Paul forced a smile, barely exposing his clenched teeth. "The Indians cut these rocks to suit their needs. Even though it's a great spot for a lookout, they disguised it to look like no one could possibly be up here. That's why every rock around here is flat on top, but doesn't look it." Only some of the clients were paying attention. Most waited for the charade to end by lying flat out across the trail. It was a fine opportunity to rest their poor legs, which had done more in the previous week than had ever been asked of them before.

"I'm pretty sure that's wrong" said the same client. "I read that the wind, rain and lightning cause the erosion that flattens out granite rocks like this one. And if this were the work of a NATIVE AMERICANS," she grunted "then there would be some visible tooling marks."

"Wow!" Paul said shaking his head "I guess you can't trust everything you read. It's a good thing you've got me here! Let's go eat lunch!"

As the group scrambled up the huge monolith some seemed to notice the faint trail that was worn into the gentle sloping edge of the rock. It was a nice surprise to those who bought into the lie sold to them courtesy of Paul. But to the suspicious others it seemed a bit too manicured. It was like a path that many people had taken. A path that Paul seemed to know extremely well even though he had "never been there." As he reached the top, Paul slowed his pace almost to a stop. Something was wrong, but the view had distracted most of the clients from Paul's ever-slowing steps.

It was obvious to him that lighting had struck the rock sometime over the winter. He slowly walked to the new edge of his final lunch spot. Peering over it he saw the 50 square feet of missing real estate lying on the bottom of the canyon, 1500 feet below. The huge chunks of granite looked to be nothing more than a pile of gravel from their point of view. But Paul knew better. He knew that there were pieces as big as truck tires. He had sat on them in the past.

Each client behind Paul was gazing out into the demanding and perilous country they had spent the week conquering. The unblinking eyes of each of them showed a mixture of accomplishment and wonder. Paul could hear the voices behind him.

"It's so beautiful," said one woman.

"It's out there somewhere," came the voice of a man.

"It seems too small for lunch."

Paul didn't look to see who had said it, but it was incredibly true. After gazing down at the rubble below, his eyes closed tightly. He could not acquiesce to the fact that he had been here just two years prior when the rock was much bigger. He had, once again, painted himself into a corner, unable to speak the truth that could keep them out of harm's way.

The rock was a huge piece of the puzzle. Horse Camp and Mexican Race Track were visible from here. It was a great place to tell the stories of how the Peralta's shipped horses into this massive confusion of bluffs and valleys just to feed the gambling addiction of their leader, Don Miguel Peralta. Music Mountain lay in the distance. It had been named when Music the dog led a search party to the skull of Adolph Ruth, the most famous victim of the Lost Dutchman's curse.

Herman Mountain, which was named after Herman Petrasch, was just beyond that. The Dutchman's unofficial, adopted stepson Rheinhart had talked his brother Herman into spending his entire life out here searching. He did, only to find heartbreak, old age, and a ramshackle home at the bottom of a small mountain, a mountain that never gave up any treasure but did take on the old man's name. The rock was a great place for Paul to re-build his authority on this range.

Just before something foolish happens, there is always that moment when it can be avoided. It's as if there is a law that states, "All stupidity shall be preceded with the absolute and unyielding opportunity to avoid said behavior." An example might be when the man says, "Watch this!" to his buddies right before he lights his homemade fireworks. Or when the wife asks her husband, "Are you sure?" the morning before he goes in to tell off his boss. The instant that the unknown client stated the obvious, "Seems too small for lunch," was that moment for the group.

And like most of those moments, it was ignored.

Paul was looking down at the scattered confusions of freshly decimated rocks on the bottom of the canyon floor below him. Soon he heard the sound of feet slipping on decomposed granite behind him. He had heard this sound countless times before. It was a swishing sound that was usually followed by the thud of easily bruised flesh striking hard granite. But not this time.

This time, the sound was followed by another set of feet slipping with no thud, then feet slipping and no thud, and so on. By the time Paul realized that everyone was catching themselves on each other, it was too late. He saw the backpack slowly rolling off the edge of the rock with its owner. The wrist lunged to move its hand towards any type of a solid hold. Paul reached for both the straps and the wrist simultaneously and caught them, only to be jerked into impending doom by the outrageous weight of the victim as it was multiplied by momentum.

The moment after he screamed his ridiculous command, "Do not let go," Paul felt as though he were sitting on the couch again on his 12th birthday. He knew there was little he could do and as the straps ripped from their stitching in the pack the sweaty wrist slipped through Paul's huge hand.

The grinding of the gravel beneath him stopped. So did time. The event didn't seem real and each client looked away. The moment left Paul holding only a small piece of nylon and his breath for what seemed like an eternity, until he heard the loud crush of death on the rocks so far below.

It seemed the curse of the mine had taken another life, the curse of an old man whose nickname was The Dutchman, a man named Jacob Waltz.

Chapter 2

The Don

-Even before you understand them, your brain is drawn to maps- **Ken Jennings**

The night hung heavy around the small adobe building like the wet saddle blanket that hung from Jacobs's mule. He felt horrible that he had pushed the poor animal so hard for so long just to arrive *here*. This nasty little building that hardly qualified as a bar was the last place either of them wanted to be.

Jacobs faced showed his deep resentment even through his thick, tobacco stained, salt and pepper beard. As the general din from inside the bar erupted with laughter, it was cut short by a small, homemade firework that went off behind the building, much too close to the ground. For a brief second the night was silent, then the laughter resumed.

"Shtop, Zicke," Jacob said in his heavy German accent. His mule, Zicke immediately stopped in her tracks. It was a welcome command from the man who had ridden her for days through countless miles of dry desert. She lowered her head for a moment then, as if her memory were jarred into life, she arched her neck hard to the left, her nose almost touching Jacobs's knee. It was a ritual that the two had gone through for years and if there were ever a time she deserved it, tonight was that time.

Jacob pulled a small piece of candy from his shirt pocket and fed it to the animal saying, "There is only one left. You must vait till ve get home for it."

"You know she doesn't speak English don't you?" Jacobs's partner said shaking his head from atop his own mule. He never understood why Jacob treated his animals the way he did. It was as if the mule was Jacob's partner and he was just along for the ride. Every time they stopped for supplies Jacob spent almost as much money on Zicke as he did on himself.

"She carries me und all my things everywhere I go, vich is more than I can say for you. All you have ever done is share my name, vich I have been meaning to talk to you about. From now on I am Jacob or Jake und you can go by your last name, Veisner."

"It's Weisner. How long are you planning on keeping that accent? Even if Zicke did speak English, she wouldn't understand you. I'm your only friend because I'm the only one who knows what you're saying. I don't really like you. How long have you lived in America?"

"That depends on vat year it is now. I arrived in 1839."

"Jake its 1867! In a month it'll be 1868! You've been learning English for 28 years! In America the language is English, and in English there is a letter W. Just like the W in the beginning of Weisner."

"Ve aren't in America now are ve? So I can speak how I vant, und I vill call you Veisner. Veisner, my second best friend, after Zicke." Jacob smiled as he dismounted, took two steps forward, put his shoulder under Zicke's chin and scratched her between her ears in what could only be described as a hug.

"Well your 'second best friend Veisner,'" the other Jake said reverting to his own natural German accent in an effort to mimic Jacob, "is about to make you a rich man."

"Ve shall see," said Jake as he tied Zicke loosely to the hitching post. He reached into his pocket and fed her the last piece of candy.

"Well if this plan works, I'll buy the next round of candy for Zicke."

"I'm sure they have more inside. Veisner how do you know he is even here? Just because you saw him here once doesn't mean much. I saw him once as vell you know."

As the words exited the bearded man's mouth there came a shout from inside the bar. It was a loud, commanding shout that would've echoed off any mountain or ridge around, had there been any in sight. It was a one word, Spanish command that the men had heard before but neither knew what it meant.

"*Callate!*" was the call from inside the bar that silenced the entire night.

"He's here." said Weisner.

"Two Germans, speaking English, valking into a Mexican bar, to steal a map to an American gold mine . . . I'm sure nothing could possibly go wrong vith this plan," Jacob said, his voice loaded with sarcasm and his head slowly shaking from side to side.

"I would hardly call what you speak English," said Weinser as he slapped the abundant dust off of his arms and chest leaving barely visible handprints in patterns on his clothes and a cloud in the air around him.

"Unt I vould hardly call this a plan. You look ridiculous," replied Jacob without even looking at the other Jake. He didn't need to look; he had seen the silly handprint pattern on Weisner's clothes at least 100 times before. He had also said the same thing to him for the last two years. It was as much a ritual as feeding candy to his mule and seemed to happen without emotion or prompting.

As they both stared briefly at the small door in the front of the building, they were each anxious about what the night would bring. Simultaneously, and without looking at each other, they both began walking towards the door that seemed to get even smaller as they approached. The loud voice from inside shouted another order in Spanish that boomed through the air.

"*Fuera de aquí!*" came the command. It was Spanish for "get out" and came as both Jakes literally ducked into the tiny doorway and entered the bar.

Within a second, they knew what was happening. The tension that each expected to be directed at them when they walked in was there, but had no bearing on either man. Instead it accumulated between two men at the faro table.

The tiny bar had three tables situated in the only manner that the room would accommodate. Two smaller poker tables on either side seated four men each. One bigger, yet still small, table in the middle of the room that seated six held the faro game.

The fourteen chairs were more a collection of driftwood and rawhide than furniture. They looked to be the byproduct of a child's effort to build machinery with only wood gathered on a remote beach. Each chair held a gambler but the one turned over near the door in which the two Jacobs had entered. Its occupant stood, with his back to the toppled chair, glaring down and across the table at a man.

It was obvious that the standing man was scared. His right knee was visibly shaking. His short breaths in followed by strong, loud breaths out sounded as though they were exiting through clenched teeth. With each breath, the man grew more afraid of his antagonist who was seated across the table. He was glaring back with deep black eyes that appeared to hold hell itself.

The seated man was holding his hat in his right hand. His greasy, unkempt hair revealed that he had just removed the hat, perhaps to give the standing man a better view into the black pits that were his eyes. His thick, dark mustache began to turn as his mouth rolled into a grimace of hatred. As each man glared into the face of the other, deciding upon their next move, Weisner whispered to Jake, "That's him, the one sitting down."

Just then the man slowly stood up. His drunkenness caused him to waver from side to side. Standing revealed a physique that was the result of hard times and heavy drinking. He was both skinny and fat, with small arms and a protruding pot-belly, yet he somehow commanded the attention of the entire bar and struck fear into the heart of the standing man. As he reached the apex of his effort, he drew back his hand and slapped the other man in the face with one, long sweeping motion. The slap turned the other man halfway around towards the Jakes.

"Seems like a vonderful guy," whispered Jacob. As the man sharply completed his turn he stepped towards the door to leave. In his rush, Jacob saw a small hole, about the size of a shot glass in the left sleeve of his shirt. It seemed an odd detail to notice in the may lay.

Stomping past the two Germans the man yelled, "*Coyote!*" to his aggressor, his courage slowly returning with every step he took away.

"*El tramposo!*" screamed the Coyote as he threw a glass, half-full of beer that struck the man's back. The man with the hole in his shirt disappeared through the same doorway that the Jakes had entered, only he didn't need to duck.

As soon as the man left all eyes turned to the two bearded men standing in the middle of the room. If tension were flowers, the room would have smelled much different. The only person not staring was the Coyote at the faro table. He looked towards his chair, began the slow process of sitting down and asked disgustedly,

"*Que quieres?*"

Jacob responded, to the dismay of Weisner, as though he understood the man.

"Ve are looking for a game of faro und it seems you are looking for a player."

"You speak Spanish, *Peludo*?" asked the Coyote, referring to Jacobs's beard.

"You don't need to speak Spanish to understand someone asking vat you are doing here."

"I asked what you wanted," The Coyote grunted without looking up to Jacob.

"It seems my English is better than my Spanish," Jake replied to the rolling eyes of Weisner. "However the answer is the same, a game of faro." Jacob reached to the overturned chair without taking his eyes off of the man. He carried it the few steps to the faro table and sat down.

"We don't play with American or German money here."

"Good, because all I have is this." said Jacob pulling a small piece of gold ore from the pocket opposite of where the candy had been. The ore had the effect of turning much of tension in the room into curiosity. All eyes were still focused on the men, only now they were struck by wonder. Even the Coyote looked up at the gold as he answered.

"My friend gold is universal, but you must know that the Peso is no longer accepted in the U.S. They began rejecting our money 10 years ago, and I don't think anyone would even know what a Peso is in your home country. Even if you win you could not spend your winnings. My friend, you have very little to gain and much to lose."

"Even a better reason to let me in the game, amigo."

"I have never been called amigo in a German accent!" the Coyote laughed hardily and brought slow laughter from the pundits, breaking the tension from the fight and the wonder from the flash of gold. His cold black stare was reduced to a squint in an effort to see through his open-mouthed laugh. "Welcome to the table my friend. Please allow me to introduce myself."

"There is no need," Jacob interrupted, "I know who you are. You are Don Miguel Peralta. Ve have met before. It was maybe 18 or 19 years ago in Arizona. It would have been Alta California to you. The war had just ended. You were at a bar north of the Gila River, about as big as this one. You vere telling your countrymen not to become U.S. citizens. You vere saying you had been robbed of your land und your fortune because you would not become a citizen. You are quite a speaker, all of the men vere listening. You said ven it came to becoming a U.S. citizen you vould rather die. Und you pointed at me und said 'or dress like him!' the people found it very funny."

"You dress much better now," said the Coyote.

"Unt you," said Jacob, trying to find a compliment somewhere in the man's appearance. It was not an easy task and after looking the man up and down he realized that hard times had certainly befallen Peralta. His clothes were little more than rags and his overall demeanor resembled that of a vagrant. As the moment became awkward, Peralta interceded.

"It seems I am an honest man! A ragged appearance is a better fate than becoming an American! My friend this is life." Peralta swept his hand across the faro table in a wide, arcing motion as if to display what was left of his dignity.

"Sometimes we win, and sometimes we lose. I am honored to find you again, only this time you hold the winning cards. It would be my pleasure to play faro with you. Please sit. Allow me to refresh myself from the unpleasantness of before. Please excuse me while I step outside. By the way, what is your name?"

"Jacob Waltz"

"Jacob Waltz, it sounds like a very important name."

"Not yet," said Jacob prophetically.

Peralta stepped around the table and past Jacob Weisner who had watched the entire exchange in horror. His face looked like an unholy union of astonishment and anger as Waltz took his seat at the table.

After a few unsettling moments, a small Mexican woman nudged a tiny chair towards Weisner. He hurriedly moved it into position next to Waltz. The chair was so small that only Weisner's head was above the top of the table.

He glared at Waltz and asked him, in a whisper, "What is wrong with you? Why didn't you tell me you knew who he was? Why would you blow our chances of stealing the map? Don't you remember we were going to wait for him to get drunk, then take the map?! Do you even know how to play faro?"

"Nothing, I did, I didn't, yes, und I do." said Waltz.

"Did you already start drinking mescal? None of that made any sense," said Weisner in what is best described as a whispering scream.

"I thought you were the only von who could understand me," Jacob smugly replied hiding a smile. "I answered all of your silly questions. Nothing is wrong vith me, I did tell you I knew who he vas, our chances of getting the map are not blown, I did remember your stupid plan, und I do know how to play faro."

"I should get on Zicke right and now lead my mule home."

"Zicke von't carry idiots, und von't lead mules without names. I guess you are stuck."

"Sorry to keep you waiting my friend," interjected Peralta upon returning from his departure. "I don't believe I learned your friend's name. Does he know me as well?"

"His name is Veisner, und he knows very little."

"Hello Veisner, *bienvenidos a México*." Peralta greeted Weisner as an adult greets a child.

Weisner was furious. Not only had Jacob stolen the spotlight, ruined the plan, and taken control of the night, but he had gotten one of the most infamous men in Mexico to mispronounce his name. He was now reduced to watching a card game from a chair that was obviously made for a child.

"My friend," Peralta blurted out, drunkenly while shuffling the cards, "where do you call home?"

"We are exploring Arizona Territory. I am a prospector und . . ." Jacob was cut short by Peralta, but not before he could place his bet. A small nugget of gold ore held his position on the seven of diamonds.

"Arizona Territory," slurred Peralta, as if it were the first time he had heard the name that night. "You have the name wrong my friend. It is *aritz ona*. It is from an ancient language. It means good oak, and it was mine." said Peralta in a low voice as he slowly dealt the cards into two piles.

"The name vas yours?" asked Jacob

"No, the place, it was mine. It was called Alta California, and it was beautiful," said Peralta as his coal black eyes looked into the space above and to the left of Jacob as if he could picture every rock and bush if given enough time. Peralta had forgotten about most of the people in the bar, and that Jacob had already mentioned Alta California when describing their first meeting.

"It still is beautiful," came the reply from Weisner which drew a look of disgust from both Peralta and Waltz as well as from those eavesdroppers in the bar who understood English.

"No! It lost much of its beauty now that it resides under that horrible flag! They cannot even decide how many stars to put on it," said Peralta to the man seated next to him who obviously didn't speak English.

"It was not so long ago that the land was Mexico. For 25 glorious years, we were a nation of our own. The newly formed Mexican government honored and respected those families who had managed and controlled property. The Peraltas were land owners, my friend! We were a proud people of, how you say, affluence." Peralta took a sip from his drink.

"This Arizona Territory that you speak of was the land for which my father fought. Armies of men died on that land in the name of Peralta. Men died who were good, who wanted a safe bountiful place for their families to grow, and we gave that to them." Peralta began to turn over the cards from one newly dealt pile, barely paying attention to the game but enthralled with his own story.

"I controlled everything. *Soy patrón*! Livestock, water, mining and everything else that happened within my boundaries fell under my control. I built cities for families and armies to defend them." Two men hollered as the next card was turned, revealing that they had placed a winning bet. But their celebration was ended quickly with a glare from Peralta.

"I was the law. I appointed judges over the people, and we were a good people. We thought our biggest enemy was the Apache. They were very easy to handle, or so we thought. We had carved out our own paradise, my friend. But it did not last long. 25 years vanished and just like that,"

Peralta clapped once, loud and hard

"it was over. *La Intervención Estadounidense* came. Gringos call it the Treaty of Guadalupe Hidalgo, but it was theft! They took my home and my people. For my people it was fine. Not much changed. They merely became citizens of another country."

The small lady who had given Weisner his chair reminded Peralta to continue dealing by nudging his hand gently. The game resumed as did the story.

"But for me, I had no more people, I had no land, I had nothing. How can the leader, *El Patrón*, turn to a humble existence next to the peasants who once served him? I could not live as a pawn on the land that I once ruled!" Peralta pounded his fist onto the table which seemed to pull him back into reality. "I went back to my mines, you know?" Waltz and Weisner looked at each other intensely. They knew

the story. It was this story that had brought them here in the first place.

"I brought my best men back with me one year before they signed the treaty. The men who were loyal to me were to be rewarded! I brought them to the Sombrero Mines. Seven fabulously rich gold mines lay on land that was soon to be stolen from me, and I could not do a thing about it. So we worked."

Peralta took another sip.

"My men worked day and night like they had never worked before. It was incredible! They worked as if there were no tomorrow because, my friend, there was not. It was the last time my men and I would see our home land for the rest of our lives! So we worked each pit until, one by one we mined each vein out," Peralta paused for another drink.

That statement made Weisner drop his head into his hands. They had ridden from the middle of Arizona territory to who-knows-where in Mexico. They had risked their lives, stepped into the middle of a fight, walked away from everything they knew for a chance to steal a map to the last remaining Peralta gold mine. Then they sat through a drunken, anger-filled story only to learn that Peralta had played each mine out before he left. Weisner was sick. As Peralta finished his drink he slowly turned over some of the remaining cards from the almost depleted stack. Then he changed everything with two words.

"Except one."

Weisner's eyes widened through his fingers. It was true! There was one left! He could not believe what he was hearing. He turned to look at Jacob and was shocked to see him stoic. The older man was almost emotionless over the entire story as if he had something else on his mind.

"We could not take any more gold my friend. Every spare space was loaded with the gold. We were determined to take what was rightfully ours from the thieves before they took it from us. Then, it happened." Suddenly, Waltz's eyebrows shot up. Up until now the story was exactly how he had heard it. Waltz had not even felt the angst that Weisner had during the short break in the story when Peralta had taken his last drink. But he had no idea that there was more.

"It was impossible to even begin on the last mine. We had more gold than our children's children could spend. But fate has a way of turning the tables, my friend." Peralta paused the game with one card left to turn.

"You know just when you think you know your enemy, another will appear. We were angry with the U.S. for stealing our land, taking what was ours to do what they want with it. It was hard for me to even remember that there were those who were there before us who felt the same way. It turned out that the Apache were ready to fight the enemy as well, and the enemy was us."

Peralta twirled a coin slowly on the table between his fingers.

"When we awoke they were upon us. Many died in their sleep. The Apaches split those of us who fled into three smaller groups. My group was the only one that made it back. My friend, I had virtually nothing left. We carried very little of the gold, most of my men were killed and I," Peralta dropped the coin, his hand hung over the final card, "I am a coward who ran from my enemy. I left my people to die in my place."

The silence was overwhelming, but was broken by the screeching of a chair. It was the chair that Waltz was sitting in screeching across the floor behind him. The same chair that had earlier been tossed out of place during the first altercation flew back. Waltz stood and jumped towards a man who was standing curiously close to Peralta. It seemed that the entire room was listening to the story, intently focused on Peralta, with the exception of two men. One, whose hat covered his face who had slowly made his way into the bar and up to the table. The other was Waltz, who had watched the man out of the corner of his eye.

As Peralta slowly and quietly uttered his last sentence, Waltz watched the man reach into his belt for a knife with his left hand revealing a hole, the size of a shot glass in his newly purchased, dirty shirt. Waltz knew immediately that it was the man who Peralta had slapped as the two Jakes walked through the tiny door.

As he lunged at the man, the assailant's old seat was thrown across the room by the back of Jacobs's legs. Jacob caught the man's wrist in one hand and his hair in the other, his bodyweight crushing the smaller man to the ground. While the man screamed obscenities in Spanish, Jacob pinned the arm holding the knife to the ground with his knee. He shoved the man's face to the dirt floor with his left hand and controlled the other arm with his right.

Each person in the room sat, breathless as the incident ended almost before it began. Weisner and Peralta seemed to be the most awestruck as they both shared a look of complete shock. Neither had changed their position at the table, only turning their head slightly towards the commotion.

"I vould like some help please," plead Waltz jarring the others into action. Two of the gamblers from the faro game and one man from a poker table took control of the would-be murderer. As the man was hauled out of the bar he screamed, "Coyote!" over and over. Waltz took his seat from its new position in the middle of the room and replaced it at the table again, straightened the hat that had remained on his head during the altercation, and sat down.

"My friend you have just saved my life. I...I do not know how to thank you."

"Vell, you could start by turning over the last card." Waltz flashed a smile that was hidden by his beard, but showed in his eyes.

"Gladly, but first I want to offer you something. My friend, it seems that fate has brought you here tonight to listen to my sad story. The game," Peralta said with another sweeping motion of his hand over the undisturbed table, "has brought you here for a reason. I can only give you this. Please my friend it is all I have. I can do nothing with it now, and it will never repay the debt I owe you but please take it."

Peralta reached into the inner pocket of his vest and pulled out an old, supple, yellow piece of leather. Weisner's eyes widened as he looked at what could only be the map. The purpose of the entire trip lay in front of them and came forward in such an unbelievable way that he was speechless. He turned his awestruck stare towards Waltz. The favor was not returned.

"You say you live in the *aritz ona*. Are you familiar with the *Rio Sal*? It is south of, I'm sorry I don't know the English words. *Cuatro Puntas*," said Peralta slowly opening the map.

Jacob had no idea what the *Rio Sal* or *Cuatro Puntas* was until he saw the map. Immediately he recognized the Salt River that ran south of Four Peaks mountain range. He had travelled up and down the river many times. It was a strange river that tasted like the ocean but had fresh water fish in it. Many times he had camped there but much further down from where the map referenced.

"Yes I know of it, but further down is my home," replied Jacob.

"My friend, this map will take you to the last of the seven Peralta mines. There is one X remaining of the original seven. I have covered over the other six with my own blood as each mine played out," Peralta looked into Jacob's eyes for reassurance that using his own blood on the map was appropriate. By the look on Jacob's face he could tell the old German felt uneasy.

"There is no trail, only waypoints. You can see that *Cuatro Puntas* will line up with *Sombrero Grande* and form a line over the mine. It is the only north/south canyon within that line. Please, my friend, honor me by taking this small payment. It is all I have. It seems that the game has taken the rest from me. If I had more to give, I would."

"I vould like one more thing, und vee can be even."

"My friend I told you, I have nothing else. I have gladly given you all I have." Peralta said in a voice that was a mixture of anger and frustration.

"Please, amigo one last thing," Waltz paused for much too long, allowing the discomfort of the room to build along with Peralta's embarrassment. Then, in his harsh accent he once again derailed the tension in the room by saying, "I vould like to finish the game."

Peralta had forgotten about the game for basically the entire time he had dealt it. He smiled at the simple request of the old man and the symbolic way in which this eventful, yet short night was going to end. He slowly turned the old, yellow symbol of fate and revealed the card that would determine the final winner of the night. The man with his money on the seven of diamonds had won the final turn. That man was Jacob.

"It appears the last card is the seven of diamonds, much like the seven Peralta mines of my younger days. My friend, it looks like you will have to find a way to spend those pesos after all." Peralta pushed a pile of pesos in the direction of Waltz.

"It is OK amigo, I don't think I vill need them." With that Waltz picked up his ore and left the pesos on the table. The two men stood up, shook hands and turned to leave. Just before they reached the undersized door, Weisner spoke up from his still seated position on the tiny chair.

"*Sénior*?" cracked his voice in a questioning manner.

"Yes?" said Peralta, confused at the sudden interest from the man who had said almost nothing all night. "Do you know where I can buy some candy for a mule?"

Chapter 3

A Grave

*-There is nothing more difficult to take in hand, more perilous to conduct, or more uncertain in its success, than to take the lead in the introduction of a new order of things -***Niccolo Machiavelli**

The thunderous boom caused everyone around the white van to flinch, except Paul. He continued to peel an apple that looked more like a rose colored racquetball in his huge hands. The smirk crept across his face as he watched the entire group flinch. Jumpy clients were easy to fool. He looked up at the clear, blue sky trying to find the thunder cloud that had released the explosion.

"What in the world was that?" asked Willis Washington. Though the boom had startled him, he continued to smile as he spoke through the dignified lines at each corner of his mouth. The dark, mocha color of his skin offset the brilliant whiteness of his teeth. His strong, wiry biceps peeked out from the almost ratty tee shirt that slipped up his arms as Willis reached for his jacket.

"Don't you have lightning back in Grand Bay Alabama?" asked Paul.

"Why, yes we do, that's why I asked what that was, because it most certainly wasn't lightning." He said, finishing with a huge smile and an air of confidence.

"I'm with Willis, that wasn't no lightning. It was one of them sonic booms from an airplane" said Taylor Beaumont. The lone star belt buckle he was wearing gave away his Texas origin much more subtly than his accent did. Just as he opened his mouth to speak, his son Steven chimed in. Taylor rolled his eyes.

"That sonic boom was louder than crinkled up newspaper in a trash can."

Paul squinted confused. "Of course a sonic boom is louder than crinkled up newspaper in a trash can Steven, so is lightning which is what that was." Paul took a step closer to Taylor and quietly asked. "Taylor what is up with your boy and his sayings that never make sense?"

"Oh," Taylor said, easily loud enough to Steven to hear, "he thinks he'll come up with some great, new one-liner that people will be using for the next hundred years or so. So far he ain't come up with even one that's worth saying once! He gets it from his momma. She's too bright neither."

"She must be dumb to stay with you all these years. Or she feels sorry for you. 'Poor 'ol man' says she 'who'll show him where his glasses are or teach him how to make sun tea if I go? " The laughter in Stevens's voice didn't take the sting off of what he had said.

"Well it sure wouldn't be you. I know that. If it don't happen on the computer or in a game you sure don't know about it!"

"Guys did you come out here to bicker or find the Lost Dutchman?" asked Leslie Green, her tight sleeveless shirt revealing her muscular arms and flat chest. She appeared to have been fit in the past but now seemed almost too thin. Her bright smile had shone through a look of discomfort since she arrived.

"Can't we do both? Steven what would we even talk about if we didn't bicker?"

"Well, I'd talk about how you found a barber to give you the same haircut for the last 35 years," laughed Steven.

"Well there you go; we could talk about the one time every week when I'm happy."

Jackson Tate spoke up, "Guys please, come up for air for a minute. We're out here in the middle of nowhere, just a few days from finding our fortune, with explosions going off around us and all you can do is insult each other? For all we know that was a booby trap going off halfway between us and the gold. I mean, I heard that the Black Legion still kills people out here for going after the treasure. Did you ever think about that?"

"No Jackson," animosity was pouring from Stevens' voice "I didn't think about that because I live in the real world. While you were sitting in your cozy little real estate office, looking up crazy witchcraft, I was out drilling oil wells so that America can go on being free. I'm like a freedom fighter out in the front lines of Texas. What're you? You're the office-sitter of Nevada. Office-sitting, just like…….."

"Shut up Steven," drawled Taylor. "I'm the office-sitter at our company and you work for me." Taylor had jumped in just in time to save the group from another ridiculous saying.

"It wasn't a sonic boom," the quiet statement almost shocked everyone in the group. They had forgotten Davis was even there. His quiet demeanor and even quieter voice made him very forgettable. It wasn't that the others didn't like him, he had just not said enough to give them the chance.

"I'm a well driller. Not oil wells like Steven, water wells. I hear sonic booms all day on my rig. It's about the only thing loud enough for me to hear over the engine. They echo more. That didn't echo. Not a sonic boom."

"That's right, front line well drillers, right here baby!" Steven yelled as he walked next to Davis and threw an arm around the quiet man's shoulders. Davis winced at the touch and wore the discomfort of the situation on his face, but was too shy to say anything.

Steven wasn't bright enough to notice.

"Look it wasn't the Black Legion," Paul breathed heavy, smiling through his frustration, "a sonic boom or any other wild fantasy. It was lightning. It could be storming right on the backside of Iron Mountain" Paul pointed at the giant red peak that rose above them at the trailhead "and we would never see it. It was lightning."

For a brief moment I felt a sense of tension from each person. Then Willis broke the tension with one word.

"Thunder," said Willis again smiling profusely. "Lightning don't make a noise, only thunder makes a noise."

Just as he finished speaking the sound of a small engine wafted quietly around the corner. The sound wasn't so strange, even though the group had gone most of the day without seeing another vehicle. Traffic was very sparse on the way to Rogers Trough trailhead. It was the smell that was odd.

The smell of French fries arrived almost simultaneously with the sound of the small engine and a skunky aroma, though there were no skunks around. As the group looked south towards the only road leading into the trailhead they all saw the same, small, odd looking Volkswagen van rounding the corner. It was an old van that must've been a color at one time. But now it took on the color of the literally thousands of stickers it displayed. On the top was roof rack made originally for carrying luggage but now was a compost container. As the van neared, the compost smell mixed with the aroma of fries and skunk created an olfactory experience that was unique to say the least.

"Here she is" said Paul, his voice cutting through the curiosity. The irritated look on Paul's face quickly turned to a smile when he noticed Jackson looking at him. As the van puttered to a stop at the trailhead a young woman appeared. She looked like she belonged in the mountains as most of her clothes were made of natural materials. Her shirt was a patchwork of different swathes of cotton sewn together. Her cutoff jeans draped whitened frays of denim to her knees and a hand-woven, hemp headband held her long, dirty blond hair off of her face. Willis rushed to her side.

"Why hello Miss Saffron, it's so good to see you here" the older gentleman gushed helping the young woman out of the driver's seat. As usual no one was really sure how he knew her name, including her.

"Why thank you kind sir," stated Saffron in a faux, aristocratic, southern voice "and to whom do I owe my thanks?"

"I am Willis Washington ma'am, at your service."

"Why Mr. Washington please serve me with your friendship only." Saffron giggled

Paul snorted "You know, Saffron" Paul snorted "Reavis Ranch is quite a ways form here. We are two hours late already."

"Hello Miss Saffron, my name is Taylor Beaumont, pleasure to meet you" said Taylor with his giant cowboy hat in his hand. Unfortunately his thick Texas accent made the word Taylor sound like Tyler.

"Nice to meet you Tyler" smiled Saffron.

"Not Tyler, Taylor" came his reply in an effort to clear things up, which was fruitless because the two words sounded even more identical coming from his mouth.

"I'm sorry, Tyler" said Saffron looking extremely confused. She put a heavy emphasis on the T in the hopes that it would resolve the confusion.

"No, not Tyler, Taylor, you know like Taylor Made golf clubs."

"I don't golf. Umm how about this, I can call you not Tyler, is that better?"

Taylor cursed under his breath as he walked away. "How come no one can ever get my name right, it ain't hard."

"Don't worry about dad. This happens all the time. I'm his adopted son Steven."

"I wish" yelled Taylor, who kicked a small stick in frustration over the introduction.

"Where are you from, Miss Saffron?" Steven asked with a curious emphasis on the word Miss. He was fishing for a last name perhaps but in reality wanted to know if she was single. He didn't mind the beads in her hair and even without makeup she was pretty. However his curiosity died as soon as she lifted her arms, revealing two tufts of hair that would rival his own. He hadn't looked down beyond the end of her cut off jeans to see that she hadn't shaved her legs, possibly ever. She rolled her head back, closed her eyes and exclaimed

"I'm from mother Earth!! And it's not Miss Saffron. In fact it's not Miss anything, only Saffron." Steven slowly backed away as the story continued.

"Barbara and Kyle were travelers. Barbara actually gave birth to me in our motorhome travelling from Eugene Oregon to Flagstaff. They don't remember where we were but they said it smelled like citrus."

"I doubt that motor home smelled like citrus" mumbled Paul.

"So Barbara and Kyle are your parents?" asked Leslie, smiling undeterred.

"Well they are my life-givers, but they taught me that my parents are Mother Earth and...."

"Let me guess, Father Time" gibed Paul.

"No silly, Father Karma."

"OK," Paul commanded, much louder than necessary. "I'm sure everyone got the itinerary. It said we would leave Rogers Trough by seven in the morning. It is now nine. I'm sure that Saffron has some interesting stories about her life and her," Paul swung an open hand towards Saffron's van, at a loss for what to call it. "Her, little, Earth ship. We could all talk about life-givers, eat her French fries and sing Kumbaya. But I would rather go get our fortune! Who's with me?"

As Paul's rant slowly drifted away from the group into the clear blue sky each person stood, motionless looking at Paul. They had let the moment pass without the "we're all with you Paul" holler that he had expected. Then the silence was broken when Saffron said.

"I don't even eat fries. My, little Earth ship runs on grease from restaurants."

Paul bit his own lip. "Well this trip runs on steps from hikers and I only have enough for me. Let's go."

As the group prepared the finishing touches on their backpacks and helped each other put them on Paul waded through the sea of brand new, bulging packs looking for the person with the 100 pounder. There was always one in each group who had no idea what packing that much weight around for a week was like.

In all reality each person's pack was much too heavy for them. They were all novices. But Paul knew there would be one whose pack was just ridiculous. As soon as he met Jackson Tate, Paul guessed he would be the guy. His 5'8" frame carried his 220 pound mass very well. He smiled easily. But the smile was offset by his furrowed brow and upward facing chin.

He wore every gadget that money could buy. His watch counted his steps, his pack was top of the line and brand new, and even his clothes were made from a material that seemed to intrigue the other clients. Upon arriving at the trailhead, everyone but Willis seemed very curious and wanted to feel the sleeve of his shirt.

"Jackson this is nice!" Leslie said surprised, rubbing the fabric between her fingers. "Why haven't you worn it to any of our races?"

"Oh, Ann bought it for me just for this trip. It's pretty comfortable."

"It looks expensive." Steven said unloading his pack from the back of the huge, white van.

"Well you get what you pay for." Jackson smiled and slightly raised his chin.

"What's it made out of?" Leslie walked behind Jackson and folded the back of the shirt down to reveal the tag. As the two moved in an awkward dance trying to find a label that would explain what the material was made from Willis answered the question. Without moving or looking up from his own pack he said,

"It's a polyester microfiber formula for wicking combined with a proprietary blend from Goreman Technologies. They are great shirts."

Jackson and Leslie looked at each other questioningly as the silly shirt twisting stopped. They then looked back at Willis who was wearing a faded cotton tee shirt and denim pants. His boots were worn through in some places and looked as though they would not make the trip. As he finished tying pieces of his pack together with twine he looked up at the two and smiled.

"Sounds good to me!" Leslie said, letting the tail of Jackson's shirt go, asking, "How do you know so much about these shirts Willis?"

"Oh I know a thing or two about Goreman Technologies. They are the leader in men's active wear." He grabbed his jacket, which looked like an old-fashioned lumberjack's shirt and tied it around his waist.

"Uh, that's exactly what Wes told me," Jackson looked shocked for a moment. Then, as Leslie asked him about his son, Wes he lost track of his confusion and explained how Wes was just at that age when a boy doesn't care much to be around his father. Leslie mentioned that Wes was a good kid, as if she knew him.

Then came the thunderous boom.

"Who, do you think will help you carry that pack?" asked Paul pulling the straps tight on his own pack after throwing it effortlessly on his back. With all of the confusion that Saffron had stirred up, Jackson didn't think anyone would notice him struggling under the weight of the pack. He had purposely put it on when he thought no one was looking. Fortunately for him Paul suspected he would be the guy.

Jackson looked around, then settled his focus on Paul. "I can squat 650 pounds; I know you're not talking to me." Jackson took two steps towards Paul as if to prove he was fine.

"Hmm, and how long does that take you?"

"Like 3 seconds!" uttered Jackson, proudly.

"Well we'll be hiking for about 7 hours. Now let me tell you a little secret" Paul's voice lowered to a whisper so as not to draw attention from the others in the group. "It's a whole lot easier to lighten that load here, while no one is paying attention, than it is halfway up the first switchbacks. You stop and unload your pack there and you'll have that little hippie girl rummaging around in your stuff to help" Paul put up imaginary quotation marks with his fingers around the word help "you out. I'll check on the others. I would strongly suggest you make some adjustments to your pack before we head out." As Paul turned to walk away Jackson stood tall for a moment, then slowly slid his pack off and opened the top to remove a few non-essentials.

"You know it wouldn't be so horrible if you ran veggie oil in your huge gas guzzler!" Saffron's comment came out of nowhere but was obviously directed at Paul.

"I don't think I can afford the conversion kit Saffron" Paul avoided telling clients that the van was a rental.

"Oh is that all? You just need to get into barter. I traded for all of the work to my van plus some upkeep for..."

"I don't want to know what you had to trade for that Saffron. I like things just the way they are, thanks." Paul did his best to get away from the conversation. But Saffron followed him over to Davis and continued as he adjusted the quiet man's pack.

"Would it kill you to be a little less petroleum dependent? Mother Earth only has so much to give you know."

"Saffron I'm not interested. Besides the amount of cars that had to drive to the restaurants to buy the tater tots that your fuel was cooked in probably burned more fossil fuel than what it took to make my gas."

"You don't know that. People like you always say things like that when you don't know what you're talking about."

"Well here's what I do know. I know that you paid me to take you to the Lost Dutchman's mine. I also know that I don't want a lecture on my carbon footprint the whole trip. So I know who is on head-count duty. It's you."

"What's head-count duty?" Saffron asked.

"That's the person in charge of counting heads every hour. Right now we have seven heads, not counting your own. I'd like to keep it that way." Paul smirked his trademark smile as if he had the upper hand.

"How is that supposed to keep me quiet?" pouted Saffron.

"It may not keep you quiet, but it keeps you in the back of the line. Is everyone finally ready?"

The lack of no's led Paul to the assumption that everyone was ready and seeing Jackson quickly re-entering his now lighter pack he bellowed "Let's go make our fortune!"

This time the group shouted. All except Willis, who quietly waited for the cheers to die down before saying "Mr. Paul why don't we say a quick prayer before we leave?"

"Wow, first the Black Legion and now this." Paul let out a frustrated sigh as he looked at his watch. "OK, have your prayer."

"Mr. Paul you don't pray?" For the first time the smile disappeared from Willis's face.

"There's no one for me to pray too. Make it quick."

The walk down Rogers Canyon was nice. With Paul out front leading the group down the trail each person found a rhythm. They were getting comfortable crossing the small creek that occasionally ran along the trail. Paul turned the group north to the Reavis Ranch trail and began the slow steady climb to the dreaded switchbacks.

After a short time on the trail, he turned down a very under-travelled, overgrown trail that had most certainly not been used since the last rain. He was taking the crew to his first pit stop. It was a spot which would cement his place as the aficionado of the mountain range and give the group a chance to rest before the grueling climb to the top of the mountain.

Then it happened.

Paul could hear the rustling of paper in the wind that could only be one thing. Someone had brought their own map, and that was a problem. Paul typically liked to hand out his maps at the end of the first day. Mostly because the second day was almost a complete backtrack to where the group started. So the "edited" maps did not have Rogers Trough trailhead on them. Unfortunately the map blowing in the wind behind Paul probably did.

"I thought we were going to Reavis Ranch?" Davis said in more of a questioning manner than as a statement.

"We are but I want to show you something first," said Paul. For the first time he noticed a drop of sweat running down the side of his face. He wasn't sure if it was from the hike or the tension over the map. He had to figure out a way to steal it. He knew his chance was now.

"We're here," he exclaimed trying to hide the frustration in his voice.

"You brought us to a nasty little pile of rocks," asked Taylor puffing through the sentence revealing his age and lack of fitness.

"Nope, this my friends is a grave" Paul conjured up his best showmanship as he slowly swept his arm over the confusion of rocks that were little more than a pile.

"What?" Leslie was shocked. She had been jolted into focus at the mention of the word grave. "Whose grave is it?" she asked, as her and the others began to slip out of their packs.

"This is the final resting place of Elisha Reavis, whose home we will be sleeping at tonight." The group slowly gathered in anxious anticipation for whatever story Paul was about to tell them, which was exactly what he wanted. Paul turned over a stone, revealing the rudimentary engraving on the bottom. It read "Elisha M Reavis 1826-1897".

Leslie puffed, "He deserved better," as Paul pulled up the makeshift cross that had been knocked over and placed it upright at what he had always thought was the head of the grave.

"How do you know," barked Taylor, "Shoot, he could've been some type of bank robber."

"He was not a bank robber," Paul raised his voice in a successful attempt to control the conversation. He noticed that the group had left their packs about 30 feet behind them on the trail. This was his moment, his one chance to get the map, so he devised a plan.

"Elisha Reavis came from a little town called Beardstown Illinois," Paul didn't usually tell Reavis' entire life story, though it was ingrained in him from a lifetime of hearing and reading it. He thought he knew it by heart. Every detail seemed so vivid. But like many "truths," he only knew what others had said. Some of what was the "truth" was not exactly accurate, much like the many maps to the Lost Dutchman's mine.

"He came out west in the gold rush with all the other 49ers. When things didn't exactly pan out," Paul's little pun had no effect on the group, "Elisha found himself in the Bradshaw mountains with other prospectors." Paul noticed that Leslie was staring intently at the grave. He slowly began to make his move towards the back.

"After the Bradshaw Mountains became littered with other prospectors, he moved back to California where he met the love of his life, Mary Sexton." At the mention of Reavis' wife, Jackson became hypnotized on the disorganized heap of stones.

"By 1868 the couple had their one and only child, a daughter named Louisa." Paul got this part of the story wrong. But it didn't matter because Saffron was now in some type of trance with her eyes closed rocking back and forth. Steven was intently watching her as Paul slipped behind him a half a step.

"Reavis came back out to Arizona around 1868-1869 and when he called for his wife to come out with their daughter she refused. Mary died in California a short time later, leaving Elisha out here, alone." Paul could've lit his feet on fire and turned cartwheels and no one would've noticed. He had them all fixated on the grave as he took a few small steps closer to the packs.

"He retreated to these mountains and built a small homestead. It was on sixty acres where he grew vegetables, raised beef and planted an apple orchard that still has apples in the fall. They say that in 1878 Apaches attacked him in his home. After fighting them off with his rifle they decided to wait him out. They camped out on his property, out of range, waiting for him to run out of food or water." Paul was one step from the packs now.

"He had learned a trick in California. He knew that the Indians were afraid of crazy people." Suddenly, Saffron came out of her trance and turned to shoot a disapproving look at Paul.

"Are Indian and crazy the best words you can think of? They are so harsh."

Paul tried not to look suspicious, which actually made him look more suspicious but did not reveal his intentions to Saffron.

"It's a harsh story." Saffron turned away, going back into her trance. Paul spoke in a quiet voice. "So anyway, he stripped off all his clothes and grabbed his two biggest knives." Then Paul brought the intensity back. "He came running out of his home, wearing nothing but his matted beard and long hair, waving those two knives at the Indians. They thought that anyone who would attack a camp of seven men, who were all armed by the way, had to be crazy. They turned and ran and never bugged Reavis again" Paul had reached Davis' pack and could see the map.

"They said he grew the best food around. The clear, mountain stream that fed his orchard and garden gave a different flavor to the vegetables. He'd haul them from his homestead all the way to Florence, Tempe and Mesa to sell. It was hard for folks to get fresh, mountain-raised produce in the summer those days. So he packed all the way down this mountain pushing a wheelbarrow full of vegetables just to make money. That's what he was doing when they found him," he was reaching for the map when Saffron turned again for another comment. Paul quickly sat down to mask his strange body position.

"Why would a man like that need money? If he grew everything he needed why would he be silly enough to trade it for money?"

"Because you can't grow bullets and knives," Paul said through clenched teeth. The group assumed he was frustrated with Saffron's question. They didn't know she had spoiled his efforts at stealing the map again.

"Whether you like it or not there was a lot of killing that took place up here and it didn't happen with apple cores and celery stalks." Saffron turned shaking her head again. "In 1896 he turned up missing. His friend came up here to look for him and found his body right here.

He had been partially eaten.

Some say it was wolves, others say coyotes and there are some who think it was his own dogs that done it. Either way the only option was to bury him exactly where they found him, which was right here."
Paul was now beat. He was at the end of his dramatic long story and didn't have the map. As the group slowly began to turn his way, he

remembered a poem about Reavis that he had heard over and over again. As quickly as the memory came to him so did a scheme.

"It's a tradition to recite this poem at the grave when you're here" Paul lied. "If you would bow your head while I honor this good man." As the group unwittingly gave Paul exactly the opportunity he needed by closing their eyes when he didn't even ask them to, Paul made his move. While a beautiful bit of poetry came out of his mouth, deception and theft came from his actions.

"This is Elisha Reavis, by Daniel K. Stantnekov

Near the bottom of a path, in the jagged Superstitions, Is a cairn upon a grave, of a man known by tradition

It's set within a tiny plot, a few steps from the trail, Marked by a rough-hewn headstone, made from the mountain shale

Faintly scratched and barely legible, onto the piece of slate, The name Elisha Reavis, and beneath it was the date

It was in the 1860s, when Elisha climbed those hills, And found a mountain meadow that slowed his step to still

So he paced off sixty acres, filed papers to homestead, He was miles from any neighbor, he was hermited-unwed

But the life he lived fulfilled him, as he set about his task, Fenced and cleared the meadow proper, saw deer in sunlight bask

Delighted in the pure clear stream, that ran across his land, Planted fodder for his cattle, seldom saw another man

Ponderosa kept him company, Manzanita gave him art, Rarely heard, the cougars high-pitched scream, would penetrate his heart

And one dark winter evening, he turned thoughts to spring, Resolved to plant an orchard, looked toward the blossoming

So when the snow had melted, and the days were warm again, He planted sapling apples, alongside his staple grain

Then he turned the stream of water, to sustain them through the heat, When the summer sun was burning, and the green was in retreat

His trees survived the seasons, and he saw them rooted well, In the springtime there were blossoms, in the fall the apples fell

The seasons passed for Reavis too, and finally he died, While walking upright on the trail, along the mountainside

And though his grave is in a place, few men will ever see, Each spring his apples blossom, to perfume his memory."

Paul had the map.

Each member of the party slowly lifted their head and felt a connection to the place they were going, though they had never been. Each person wanted more than anything to see the apple trees themselves. They wanted to drink from the creek in the poem and touch the ground that Elisha had tilled for so many years. Leslie shed a tear that she hoped no one had seen.

I could tell that she didn't want them to know her secret. But, as usual, Willis did.

The group was quietly motivated to march up the hill that Paul had warned them about. They each put on their packs with a resolve and newfound purpose, which was good. They were going to need it to climb up the switchbacks that lay between them and the beautiful apple orchard they were envisioning.

As Paul began backtracking down the path back towards the main trail he stopped. He felt compelled to turn and look at the grave one last time. He bit his lip, a bit sorrowful. Then he heard Davis ask, "Has anyone seen my map?"

Paul turned and flashed his con-man smile with his back to the line of people, sheepishly following him as the sorrow disappeared.

"You probably left it on the grave. Got no time to go back now. Saffron get a head-count."

"We're all here," came the faint answer from the back. "I have a question; did Elisha Reavis ever meet Jacob Waltz?"

"Nope" Paul's straight answer had a small demoralizing effect on the group, which was too bad because that was the other part of the story that Paul had all wrong.

Chapter 4

The Mine

*-I'm actually writing history. It isn't what you'd call big history. I don't write about presidents and generals...I write about the man who was ranching, the man who was mining, and the man who was opening up the country-***Louis L'Amour**

"Vat do ve have here? Elisha Reavis. Is that you?"

Jacob smiled as the crazy old man came closer. The smile seemed to infect Elisha's entire demeanor which was unique to say the least. The tall, lanky, skinny man's legs stretched almost to the ground from atop his tiny burro. The five matching animals behind him carried full, yet miniature packs that resembled those usually carried by mules.

Somehow this odd image would've looked strange with anyone but Elisha M. Reavis in the picture.

Actually he rounded out the entire package nicely. As the tiny train moved closer to the Jacobs, Elisha appeared to fade into and out of the background, as though he were part of it. He was a Caucasian man though his skin color matched perfectly the color of his clothes. It was the color of dirt. In fact it was hard to tell where his shirt sleeve ended and his wrists began because of the layer of grime that coated them both.

His matted beard faded into his midsection and conjoined the hair that hung off of his head in a thick, curly dollop that barely left room for his eyes. And, as Elisha stopped short of Waltz he stared, aiming his eyes through the two prospectors. Whether it was because they were offset by the grey, dinginess of his countenance or because of the unique coloring of them, Elisha's eyes were something to behold.

They were the only thing on the man with any color.

The blue pierced by the dark black pupil was a hue reserved only for him. There was no color like it on Earth. Just a fleeting glance from the man left many disturbed. Because of his general appearance, lack of hygiene and his almost translucent blue eyes he was easily given the reputation of being off-kilter. It was a reputation that he didn't mind and almost embraced as of recent.

But he couldn't fool Jacob.

"I'll be, you look like Jake Waltz, only older! It's been at least four years hasn't it?" Elisha cackled as he spoke, almost like the crackling of a fire.

"Evidently it vas four long years if I look half as bad as you! Do the burros still carry coffee or is that a luxury too heavy for the little beasts of burden now?"

"For you, I always have coffee, not so sure about your friend." Elisha shot a glance towards Weisner who had dismounted 15 feet from the small creek over which Waltz and Reavis were talking. He didn't consider that his mule hadn't had a drink for most of the day. His only thought was that he had to relieve himself.

Holding the reins from his mule in one hand he began to go.

Unfortunately, so did his mule, in the direction of the creek. The mule was dragging a now compromised Jake Weisner along for the short jaunt to the much needed water. All the while Weisner cursed, pulled on the reins and tried to keep his pants up. He was side stepping along with his mule in the name of decency as the other two men began laughing breathlessly.

"I see you have traded down in partners these days Jake, although he much funnier than me." Elisha managed to get out between laughs.

"He is good for a laugh unt" Jake lowered his voice so Weisner couldn't hear him and leaned into Reavis who returned the gesture "as soon as I'm done vispering laugh loudly. He vill not know vat to think." At that the two men burst into laughter simultaneously. As Weisner finished zipping up his pants he turned towards them and pouted.

"At least I would say it to your face, whatever it is." With that he looked down at a wet spot on the upper right thigh of his pants and swore, causing the two men to laugh harder than before.

"I'm camping right here tonight," said Weisner sitting down on a rock still holding the reins of his mule as it sucked in the cool, fresh water.

"I vill get some firevood. Ve must have fire, to cook coffee und dry your pants und listen to stories from my old friend Elisha." Jacob moved Zicke out of the way as Elisha led the tiny pack train across the small creek to be on the same side as the two Jakes.

"No I vill get firevood" said Weisner, mimicking Jacob "Maybe you two can find something else to talk about besides me." Weisner mounted his mule and headed out to find firewood and recover some of his fragile dignity.

"I'm not so sure you want to hear my stories Jake" Elisha said making sure that Weisner couldn't hear.

"My old friend, vat has happened?" Jacob began helping Elisha unload the packs from his mules as the men talked across the backs of the calm, tired animals.

"It's not what has happened. It's what is happening. Do you remember Mary?"

"Not so much the name but I know there vas a lady you vere communicating with."

"That's her. Mary Sexton. Well its Mary Reavis now."

"That sounds like a good story to me."

"It started that way. She was, well she is a beautiful woman. She always smiled. Just seeing her smile made me happy, a little like you old man." Elisha flashed a quick smile towards Jake that was easily returned. He let one pack saddle fall hard to the ground. "I met her family when we were in California and I couldn't stop thinking about her. She was the reason I worked so hard Jake. A woman like that deserves a good life."

"You vere von of the best at San Gabriel." Zicke shook like a wet dog as Jacob pulled off her blanket and saddle.

"Only next to you Jake. You know when you and I left California to come out here, something changed inside of me. She owned a small piece of me. I was never right while we were here and she was there. I love this place Jake. It's what California used to be. There's freedom everywhere here but I just couldn't do it without her. I never told anyone but she's the reason I went back two years ago. I went home to marry her. I thought that she was the missing piece, but when I got there I found another piece missing. It was this" with that Elisha spread his long wingspan outward which reached past both ends of his last burro in the chain.

"Not many people know but we lost a child right after the wedding." Elisha shot a curious look at Jacob. Both men knew the implications. The statement didn't faze the old German, he only listened. "It was one of the reasons we got married so fast. We were going to wait a few weeks or so and then tell people she was expecting. But before we could fake the news, she lost the baby." Elisha began sweeping clear a small piece of ground with his feet, on which he could lay out his bedroll. "Jake the day that child died she changed. Heck we both changed. I could never stop thinking about this place" he stretched out his long arms once more.

"It was calling me. Not the gold either just the land. Jake I changed inside and so did she. She never smiled again. I got a letter from her last week. There's another baby on the way, due this year. She probably didn't smile when she wrote it." Elisha stopped sweeping and looked down at the ground intensely.

"By the end of 1868, I'll either be a father or have lost two children in one year of marriage. If they make it, I'm bringing them out here. I can't stay sane in California but I can't stay sane without Mary either. I need her, here, in this place, Jake. There are only two things in this life that I need. That's why I'm here." Jacob reached over one of Elisha's saddles. He pulled a dingy old bedroll across the worn leather and handed it to Elisha, a reminder to keep working. Elisha continued, "To build Mary the finest ranch I can with all the comforts of home. I know how to get her out here too Jake. She loves apples. I'll have the best apple orchard in the territory. Then she'll come."

"That does not sound like a sad story to me. It sounds like the sad part of a vonderful story! But my friend vere in the world vill you find a place to grow apples here. It is awfully varm for apples."

"Jake, it's here, somewhere. There's a place here for me. You know the older I get the more it seems that there is a spot for me, all I have to do is find it."

"My friend I can tell that wisdom has come along with your age. As

long as you are wise, you can continue to remain so ugly!" With that Jacob slapped Elisha on the shoulder. Both men laughed.

Elisha rolled out a pile of dirty blankets and cotton. The bedroll had taken on the same color and odor as Reavis from years of use, without washing. "Jake, look over there, do you see what I see?" Elisha pointed over Jacobs shoulder.

"Do you mean the giant dead mesquite tree full of firevood?"

"Yeah that's what I mean. Didn't your partner go that way for firewood?" Reavis pointed in the opposite direction of the tree.

"Yes, und if you knew him you would know that's exactly vat to expect from him."

"Why do you keep him around?"

"You just said there is a place carved out in the vorld for us. His place is here, with me. Sometimes, vell, many times he makes bad decisions, but he is a good man. Und he has led me to a very interesting point in my life."

"He....has led you?" Elisha's bushy eyebrows rose up as he questioned the previous statement. Both men began to break pieces of the standing dead mesquite tree for firewood. Under the thin dying shadows produced by the bare branches of the dead tree that crisscrossed each man's face, Jake said one sentence that shocked Elisha.

"Elisha, he found the Don."

"Oh Jake, don't tell me you're trying to find the last Peralta mine. You know as well as I do that Miguel Peralta is a crook, a thief, a coward and a terrible gambler. To be honest I'm not sure he's still alive. Did you know that two years ago the Apaches ran him out of here? He was trespassing on American soil in Apache land." Waltz was a bit shocked that Reavis had known about the raid and he had not, though he didn't let on.

"Elisha this vas his land first, und ven the Apaches ran him out of here, his men had mules loaded vith gold. Und he is alive, und gambling, or at least he vas a month ago. I played faro with him."

Reavis' eyes peeled open.

"Jake you played faro with Don Miguel Peralta? And people say I'm crazy." Elisha shook his head. "If you are telling a story to me, you don't have to. I like you already. If you are telling the truth, then you are, as your friend Peralta would say, loco. Jake he is a very powerful man who lives and dies by the game! He has killed people over a lot less than a gold mine. How on Earth did you manage to find......"

Just then they heard Weisner swearing at his mule, which was crow-hopping away from the cat claw bush tied to his saddle horn.

"There's no mesquite anywhere. We'll have to burn this nasty cat claw but at least it's something."

"He is how," said Jake in an answer to Elisha's unfinished question.

"Well, I hope you won big Jake."

Weisner noticed the two men standing under the dead mesquite tree with armloads of firewood just a few short feet from camp. He swore under his breath. Then he saw Waltz drop his armload of wood, reach into his pocket and pull out the map from Peralta. Weisner swore again, only this time loud enough for the other two men to hear it.

"What are you doing? That is our future Jake. If you want to gallivant around and poke fun at me to your friends that's fine but that is our map, not yours. I don't know who this pole cat smelling old man is.

What makes you think you can just show that to anyone you want? I seem to remember being the guy who located that map."

"Yes, und I seem to remember being the one who got the map without getting our necks cut."

Elisha glared at the map during the entire argument then, without lifting his gaze, put all questions to rest with one comment.

"I'm not interested in gold. Show me a map to an apple orchard and I'll be interested. The money isn't in the gold." Jacob, slowly put the unfolded map back in his pocket as Reavis finished his sentence.

"Wow, your friend is off his rocker. The money isn't in the gold? You are as nuts as you look." Weisner pointed a finger in the face of Reavis. As both men glared at each other, Weisner secretly hoped it would end soon. Elisha's eyes were cutting through him when the tension was broken by Waltz.

"He is right you know." Weisner snapped his head in the direction of Waltz, partly at the shock of the statement but mostly to get away from the ice cold glare of Elisha Reavis, which was still aimed at the side of his face. "Perhaps if you vould listen you might learn something. Do you know vy the Lord gave us two ears und only von mouth?"

The statement and question from Jacob shocked Weisner. He could not believe what he was hearing. Jacob Waltz, the man who became a citizen of the United States just so he could own legal gold claims, was agreeing with the man who said, "The money isn't in the gold."
As he stammered out a reply, all he could come up with was,

"I...uh...it...uhh, No.....I don't."

"So ve can listen twice as much as ve speak. Let us build a fire und my friend Elisha can tell you vy the money isn't in the gold over a nice cup of coffee, hmm?"

The crackling fire made the only sound in camp for quite some time. All three men sat, silently watching the black, greasy pot of coffee sit stagnant on the coals, not yet boiling. Even the coyotes and mules were silent. Each man wanted something different to come of the ensuing conversation, but none wanted to start it. The night was waiting for something to happen and until it did, silence dominated.

"What in the world do you mean you played faro with him?" Elisha's question brought relief to each man, breaking the quiet somberness of the night.

"Exactly vat I said. I played a game of faro with him. I von, you know."

"What is that crazy Mexican doing back here? He should know this ain't his home anymore."

"He wasn't here. We went there. Jake and me went to Mexico. He played Peralta in a little bar that I found, that I learned Peralta visited and that I took Jake to." Weisner tried hard to stake his claim as the equal partner in the relationship with his statements. His emphasis on each I left no one speculating what he was actually saying.

"Jake, why would you follow this nimrod all the way to Mexico for something as silly as a map to a mine that may not even exist? Just because Apaches killed some Peralta Mexicans with gold in their packs doesn't mean anything. That two-faced gambler probably loaded those poor men down with gold from Mexico and sent them off to be killed by Apaches just to throw people off the scent of his real mine. I really can't believe you're tied up in this.

"I didn't vant to go!"

"What?" Weisner's jaw dropped

"I also thought is vas a goose chase. But Veisner needed me. He told me his plan to steal the map from Peralta. I knew that would be the death of him. I vent to help him keep his own skin. Elisha you said our job is to find the place that fate has carved out for us. My friend this map came to me. I did not come to it. I don't understand vy but fate has chosen me…….along vith my friend Veisner."

Weisner felt the strange combination of loyalty and betrayal running through his mind.

"How does a treasure map fall into one's lap?" Reavis asked.

"Vell, Elisha the thing is, vell, I saved his life." With that, the coffee began to slowly bubble.

"What? You saved Don Miguel Peraltas life? Last month? In Mexico?" Reavis stammered

"That is correct."

"So if your buddy here didn't drag you into Mexico, then Peralta would be dead?"

"Yes," answered Waltz.

Reavis pointed his silence directly towards Weisner.

"Seems your friend here" Weisner avoided the icy cold glare from Reavis, "has a problem with gold."

"No, I just have a problem" Reavis loaded the last word with sarcasm, "with the dumb things that dumb people do for gold."

"Wasn't it you who said 'The money isn't in the gold'?" Weisner smiled prematurely at his upcoming wit. "It was less than 20 years ago that a half a million people headed out to California because there was money in gold."

"Yeah, dummy, and I was one of them! That's why I know where the money is!" Reavis leaned closer to Weisner as the volume of his voice grew.

"Well just because you didn't get any doesn't mean it wasn't there. You probably scared the gold away with your smell!"

Both men stood up as the coffee began to boil over the side of the soot-covered pot.

Waltz quickly grabbed two forked sticks and pulled the pot off the coals while saying "Enough! Jake sit down! It is time for you to shut the hole in the bottom of your face und listen. Elisha I vouldn't allow someone to say those things about you. Veisner is my friend. You may think vat you vant but keep the insults to yourself."

Jake reached into his pack as the men sat down. He threw each man a small cake wrapped in cloth. "Here are some cakes I have been saving. I vill pour the coffee now und I expect two things. Veisner shut your mouth und open your ears. Reavis, tell Veisner vat you meant ven you said 'the money is not in the gold.'" Weisner unwrapped his cake fiercely and took a huge bite from it. Elisha sat his cake down, still wrapped and said

"The money is not in the gold. It's around the gold." Weisner grunted as soon as the words left Reavis' lips. But before he could speak Waltz hit him with a rock in the shoulder, picked up another one and said

"The next one is in the ear."

"Do you know who started the gold rush of '49?" asked Reavis

"Yeah, it was John Sutter and James Marshall."

"Nope. The gold was found at Sutters Mill but they weren't the ones who started the gold rush. Think about it, why would John Sutter want every idiot with a pickaxe digging up his gold?" Waltz dropped his rock when he saw the change on Weisner's face.

"I guess they wouldn't."

"Son I got there a little late, like most folks did. Back in Illinois all we heard was how much gold was in those mountains that America just got from Mexico. You could just show up with a bag and take as much as you could carry the way we heard it. All we had to do was show up. Everything we needed was there."

Reavis picked up his cake but didn't unwrap it.

"Well sure enough half of that story is true. Once I got there everything I needed was there. I bought a pair of trousers from a man named Levi Strauss, I ate meals cooked by a lady named Luzena Wilson. I found out later that she owned the room I was renting. You heard me right SHE owned the building. But mostly I bought all my supplies from a man named Samuel Brennan. He had the finest store I had ever seen. Everything was there. You see this camp?"

Waltz handed each man a hot cup of coffee as Elisha pointed at the various packs lying around the fire. Without waiting for a response from Weisner he exclaimed

"At least half of it came from Brennan's store. After I got outfitted I took to the creeks. I worked that water as hard as I ever worked anything in my life. I watched prospectors come and go and I kept working, believing that all I had to do was work hard and the jackpot would come. I found some placer gold, enough to keep me fed but after what seemed like an eternity it hit me. People work hard every day and don't succeed. I could dig a hole to China and if there wasn't any gold in it, it would just be a hole."

Reavis put down the cake.

"I was a beaten man. I packed up my camp and headed out to find a job teaching. I wondered how it was that word had gotten out so fast about the discovery of the gold but not of the slow decline. Then I learned something. The man who owned the newspaper at the beginning of the rush was Sam Brennan." Even Jacob looked surprised at this revelation.

"He told the stories that brought the people to his stores needing supplies. Did you know that the first millionaire from the gold rush was Brennan? He made more money selling goods to miners than almost all of the miners did put together. The man I bought my trousers from got rich, the lady who cooked my dinners got rich but I . . ." Reavis paused,

"I just got older. That's why I'm telling you the money is not in the gold," Reavis sipped his coffee and shook his head, "it's around the gold."

"You know me and Jake worked together don't you. We worked the San Gabriel River in California, came out to here together with Pauline Weaver and," Elisha paused in thought, "what was the other guys name Jake?"

"Peeples," answered Jake who was looking, somewhat reminiscent.

"That's right Peeples. I always told him he spelled his name wrong. We worked a lot together in the Bradshaw Mountains and do you know what we have to show for it? Nothing. People like Strauss and Brennan have every nickel I ever made. I might as well have worked for them." For a short time Reavis let up, but not for long.

"And now you," Reavis shot an ice cold glare towards Weisner, "have my friend out here chasing some crazy fantasy. Maybe it is real, but even if you do find it, you'll just be the men who pull the money out of the ground for someone else; or the men who died trying."

Weisner didn't know what to say. He sat speechless staring at the ground in front of him. For the first time he was lost for words. Then, Jacob said it for him,

"He doesn't have me out here Elisha. I'm out here on my own. You should know better. You said yourself each man must find the spot carved out for him. This is my spot."

"How do you know?" asked Reavis.

"The same vay you know this is your spot. You belong here as do I. We just belong here in different vays."

"Maybe that's true. Either way, Weisner, you don't have to worry about Jake showing me your precious map. It may as well be a map to a dung heap for all I care. In fact I don't want to see it. But let me give you a little advice Jake."

"Unt vat would that be?"

"Never let Weisner hold the map."

"Vy not?" questioned Jacob

"If it was in his pocket today, it would be soaking wet!" Jacob and Elisha belly laughed for at least 30 seconds before Weisner slowly joined in. The three men continued to talk for the rest of the night until finally the fire let them down in the early hours of the morning.

"How can you sleep that vay?" asked Jacob shaking Weisner's shoulder with the bottom of his boot. Weisner had fallen asleep on his side, stretched over a rock with his waist at the peak of the stone. This put his hip bone higher in the air than his head or feet.

Weisner rolled off the rock onto his back. He was shaking off the early morning air and opening his eyes to the image of Waltz and Reavis looking over him from each side as though he were a corpse.

"If I had known you two were watching me, I wouldn't have been sleeping. . . I'd have been bathing."

The only upper hand Weisner had on the two was hygiene. He did a fair job staying clean compared to his partner. And most animals were cleaner than Reavis.

"I don't think he was asleep, I think he was lying there watching us put camp away with one eye shut." Elisha threw Weisner's bridle at him. As it landed heavily on his torso as he looked around. Camp was broken. It looked exactly as it did when they ran into Reavis the day before. Weisner began to sit up and prepare himself for the day by patting his clothes leaving his signature hand prints everywhere.

"He's like a blister, he shows up after the works done." Waltz smiled at Elisha's joke. "So Jake I don't care where the X is on your map but I sure would like to know the general area you'll be in, just in case I see some crazy prospector headed your way I can run him off."

"You know I vould tell you exactly vere ve vill be don't you?" asked Jacob.

"Of course I know you would but honestly Jake, that's something that I don't want to know. I don't want that draw on me anymore. I'm not planning on finding the mother lode. I plan on selling vegetables to the ones who do. Knowing where you're going would be a constant pull on me to do the wrong thing. The sooner I can get a homestead going, the sooner I can get Mary out here. Just give me an idea."

"You remember the old Peralta headquarters?" said Jake knowing full-well that Reavis knew the giant cave with the stone house inside.

"Of course I do."

"Straight north of there."

"You're pretty close now. Well, I hate what you're doing, but I'm sure glad that you're doing it crossed our paths again. Keep this vagrant close. He'd never make it without you." Elisha nodded at Weisner without looking at him.

"Yeah, it was great to meet you," Weisner quipped. "Hopefully we will see you soon, after you're stuck in a long, heavy downpour, in a field full of heavily scented wild-flowers."

Elisha left, leading his tiny train of burros, feet near dragging the ground, looking for a place to build a life for Mary.

As the two Jakes crossed the small stream where they had met Elisha the day before Jacob gave Zicke the token piece of candy while the sure-footed animal never missed a stride. Weisner sheepishly asked Jacob a question.

"Jake why do you carry the map? We have been riding for at least a month since Mexico and I haven't seen the map for more than twenty minutes. Reavis is right. You don't trust me. You don't think I wouldn't make it alone, would I?"

Waltz closed his eyes slowly, thinking about what his answer would be. As Zicke's slow, smooth rhythm caused Jakes head to sway back and forth he answered Jakes question with a question.

"Vat do you think Veisner?"

"Sometimes I'm not sure. You know I……"

Before he could finish his sentence Jacob stopped him.

"Unt that is vy. Veisner I trust you, but you vould have a hard time alone for awhile because you aren't sure. Veisner have you ever seen me make a mistake."

"Well sure, not very often, but yeah. There was that time….."

"I do not need a recollection. A simple yes or no vill do."

"Then yes."

"Now after the mistake, did you see me get frustrated, or act like a vischer or throw a fit?"

"No, I can't say I have."

"That is because I know it is OK to make a mistake, as long as you learn from it. I expect to make mistakes. Veisner you try so hard to be perfect that when you do stumble it ruins the whole day." Weisner's mule stumbled.

"Then you become frustrated, you can't think right und then you make another mistake und then, you become unsure. Veisner mistakes are expected, but frustration is your enemy. The only thing I do for you is calm you down, after that you can think again."

"Jake I know that I get worked up, and I know that sometimes you have to think but other times you have to go and do. I am a do-er."

"That is true. You do while I am thinking. Und that is vy ve make such a great team!"

"Good, then the next thing I will do is carry the map." Weisner smiled and held out his hand.

"That is perfect, as soon as I am done thinking, you can carry the map."

Both men laughed as Weisner drew back his hand and shook his head.

The conversation carried on and the two men talked about many things. As the miles carried on the men almost forgot about where they were going and they let the mules take control.

As they climbed up a high saddle in the later hours of the evening Jacobs face changed entirely. He looked ahead, towards the north, then back to the south, then to the north and back south again. While Weisner continued on with the conversation Jacob reached into his pocket and slowly pulled out the soft leather map. Zicke continued walking even when Jacob dropped the reins in an effort to use both hands to unfold the map. Then, in a moment of eureka, Jacob interrupted Weisner with three words that changed the course of history.

"Ve are here!"

"What do you mean Ve are here?" Weisner could hardly contain his excitement but still felt a twinge of disbelief.

"Look ahead that is Cuatro Puntas, Four Peaks."

"I only see one" blurted out Weisner confused.

"It is because they are in a line, one behind the other. Und behind us El Sombrero."

As the men turned in their saddles they could see the monster 1000 foot spire.

It was Weavers Needle.

Jacob continued to scan the horizon until he found the edge of the mesa which ran in a north south direction and dropped straight off, into a canyon below them. When the two men rode to the edge and dismounted the sun was beginning to creep below the red bluffs behind them. But it was giving them enough light to see the obvious tailings pile and abandoned camp that was directly below them.

"Peralta vas true to his vord. This must be the last of the seven Peralta mines."

"Well what are we waiting for? Let's go!" Weisner was so excited that he could hardly get back on his mule. He was trying for the third time to put his foot in the stirrup when Jacob stopped him.

"Ve vill never make it. The sun is already down Veisner. Ve must make camp here tonight." Weisner began to wrinkle his face in frustration but then, as if remembering the talk from earlier in the day he smiled and said

"We did it! Tomorrow we will be rich men!"

"Tomorrow, everything changes und the hard vork starts" Jacob said with a smile.

"Well good. If everything changes maybe tomorrow I can carry the map!"

Chapter 5

A Tree

*-The thing that is really hard, and really amazing, is giving up on being perfect and beginning the work of becoming yourself-***Anna Quindlen**

As Paul waited at Reavis saddle he was impressed with the speed in which the group had followed him up the switchbacks. The 700 foot elevation gain usually put his client's 40 minutes behind him. But looking down the trail at this new batch of "city-ots" he realized that they were probably less than 30 minutes from catching up.

This was the spot where he rehearsed the speech he would have to give at the end of the trip, explaining how someone had come in and stolen the ore without filing the proper claims. He would even act mad and kick or throw something during his practice run because it was impossible for the group to hear or see what he was doing.

He was all alone, or so he thought.

He counted seven people in the group, from his hiding spot. They were easy to see though the branches of an oak tree that stood on the edge of the beautiful overlook. He could see Leslie out front; sweat pouring off of her determined face, conquering the trail more that hiking it. Jackson took the position after her and was trying to hide the fact that his pack was still too heavy. It slowed his steps even after taking out his extra camp stove, camp chair, camp shower and accidentally leaving behind his first aid kit at the trailhead.

Davis was close behind and although he looked somewhat tired, his demeanor hadn't really changed. He wasn't smiling or frowning he was just existing as he walked. There was an expansive gap that separated them from the rest of the group and as Paul watched he could see that Willis and Saffron were trying to help Taylor up the switchbacks while Steven mocked him.

Obviously running the multi-million dollar oil company had removed the once strong man from the work that had kept him physically fit. He had turned into with what Steven had called Jackson earlier in the day, an office sitter. With all heads accounted for Paul launched into his rant, though somewhat under his breath due to the closeness of the group, because he thought no one could see or hear him.

He had no idea that I was even there.

"We've been beaten! I've worked my whole life for this one moment and now" Paul lowered his eyes for a dramatic effect "now it's gone."

The anguish with which he rehearsed the speech could have been an outtake from Gone with the Wind. He could have placed the back of his hand on his forehead and fainted. Instead he looked up from his pathetic pose and flashed his familiar grin that showed just how proud he was of his own talent.

Reavis saddle is a beautiful place. It is there that the trail opens up from a thick, dense, sightless, uphill treachery of thorns and thistles to a wide open, flat, resting spot. There is a breathtaking view of the amazing wilderness beneath it. It gives hikers the first glimpse of the inviting forest that shelters the Reavis homestead and signals the beginning of the downhill hike into Reavis Ranch.

It is also the place where Taylor puked.

"Dad that's grosser than cleaned up road kill" Steven stole the concern the group had for his father for a moment with his attempt at wit.

"Why don't you keep making up stupid things to say instead of helping me get this pack off my back?" Taylors drawl punctuated the sentence with sarcasm beautifully. "Heaven forbid you do anything to help me die comfortable" which signaled round two of the purge.

"Oh you won't die from puking. It'll be your heart. That old thing will never make this whole trip" Steven nudged Davis with his elbow and smiled before Davis could take a couple of uncomfortable steps away.

"Here," said Leslie as she removed her pack, grabbed her water and made her way next to Taylor in one swift movement" get some water in you, slowly. Sit down on this log and I'll help you take your pack off." Leslie fired a bitter look Stevens's way with a newfound concern for Taylor's health.

"Thank you Miss Leslie, you're a sweetheart."

"Here you go, not Tyler" Saffron was apparently still not sure of Taylor's name "take some of my granola."

"Miss Saffron you are a peach, even if you don't know my name."

"Don't do anything too slowly. Our little time delay" Paul said flicking his thumb towards Saffron "put us behind schedule. Get rested, grab a snack and let out whatever needs out here. I've got something important I want to show you." Paul had set up his next lie so beautifully that it almost told itself.

"What is it you want to show us Mister Paul?" Willis asked, somewhat strangely.

"It's the world's biggest juniper tree!" The lie left Paul's lips with ease. After a small break each hiker was somewhat excited to see the world's biggest juniper tree. They questioned each other, mentioning Sequoia National Park and The Redwood Forest wondering how on Earth the world's biggest anything was growing out here in the desert.

As the group passed Honeycutt Spring Saffron called out, "All heads accounted for sir!"

"Okay Saffron, I got it." Paul said with a shake of his head and a small smile on his lips.

"Sir, just doing my job, sir" Saffron topped off her reply with a salute that no one but me saw because of her position in the back of the line. But it made her feel good.

"Uhg, why would you mention that word?" Jackson's disgust came out of nowhere.

"What word?" asked Saffron.

"Job, isn't that what we all came out here to get away from?" Jackson pretended to gag a little as the word job left his lips.

"That's what happens when you're an office-sitter..." Stevens's sentence was cut short as Jackson turned around, stopping the flow of traffic behind them, and ending up face to face with his antagonist.

"Do you know that I made $2.5 million 'office-sitting' last year? I'm one of the few people who can bring money home from Vegas." With his nose almost touching Stevens top lip he continued to move his muscular frame forward, into Stevens's space.

"Look Tex, I don't know what you made last year, saving America," Jackson poured on the sarcasm, "on your oil rig. But I'd bet that even if you added your income with daddy's money you wouldn't have half the bank account that I have. So why don't you back off?" Jackson

"If your money is so great then how come you're so miserable earning it? "Stevens question shot through Jackson. He stood motionless, unable to reply. Taylor stepped between the two men.

"Steven shut your mouth. I buy property all the time from folks like Jackson. If it weren't for men like him you wouldn't have a place to park that rig on. Now shut up and have a little respect."

"He's right." Jackson straightened out his pack and, noticing that Paul and Davis had not stopped for the commotion, began walking fast

trying to catch up. He left the scene with one last comment, "My money is miserable." The group was now in shock following close behind Jackson.

"I got into real estate to make money, I don't like my job. I hate it. Honestly, I wish I felt as proud of my job as Steven does." Jackson left a wake of surprise in his hustle to catch Paul and Davis.

"Well even squirrels like peanut butter." Steven said, in the may lay of the group keeping up with Jackson.

"Steven, you could screw up an anvil, you know that?" Taylor was disgusted as he continued. "Jackson sometimes we do what we don't like for our families. I'll bet your family has a great life." Taylor smiled, trying to pick up moral.

"Not really" was all Jackson could say.

"Hurry up. The world's biggest juniper tree might die before you get here" Paul joked from around the corner.

The trailing group walked around a small bend in the trail and saw the tree. It was a shame that such a magnificently huge tree was the source of such a silly lie. Davis was looking straight up with his jaw hanging open which was strange because the tree was only tall for its species. Compared to the swaying pine trees around it, it was average. Its size came from the girth of its trunk. As the group approached the tree Jackson sat in a small patch of grass, far enough away from the tree to be somewhat alone but still within eyesight.

"Leslie, grab my hand" Saffron reached out to Leslie and began to form a human chain around the tree by grabbing Davis' hand as well. Davis was shocked for a moment but, oddly smiled and took a few steps closer to the tree.

"Come on not Tyler, get in here" said Saffron.

"It's not, not Tyler its, uh. . ." Taylor's voice faded away as he realized that he had no way of telling Saffron what his name was in a way that she would understand. He grabbed her hand, smiled and reached out his other hand saying.

"Come on Steven, it's the only time I'll ever give you a hand out."

"That's the truth" said Steven, smiling. He reached his other hand out and grabbed Leslie's, completing the human ring around the tree. Although no one in the ring was pressed hard against the giant landmark, the ring could not have been completed with just four people. It was a huge tree that demanded a level of respect. Saffron respected it in her own way saying,

"Yay, you're all tree-huggers now!"

"I'm out," said Taylor, immediately dropping Davis and Steven's hands. As the group around the tree laughed and talked, Jackson sat quietly in his spot, reflecting. He never even heard Willis sit down behind him until Willis asked.

"Jackson, do you know how tall a tree will grow?"

Somewhat startled Jackson smiled when he realized that it was Willis asking the question.

"I don't know, I guess it depends on a lot of different things."

"No, not really, every tree grows the same amount."

"That can't be true. I mean look at the world's biggest juniper tree" at that he rolled his eyes showing early signs of disbelief in Paul "it's bigger than all the other trees."

"No sir, I'm afraid it isn't."

"How so?" Jackson was genuinely interested in the frustrating conversation.

"Well each tree grows the same amount because they all grow as big as they possibly can. Trees never grow less than what they are capable of. So this giant juniper is the same size as that small oak over there. They are both as big as they can be, no less, no more."

"Well I guess you have a point. You know that's all that I have ever tried to do in my life is grow as big as I can. I've spent my entire adult life getting bigger and bigger. My career, muscles, houses, you name it, and I grew it. You know I think it ruined me. I guess that's why I'm not a tree."

"Well one thing I know is that a tree will be as big as it possibly can, but it will always be the same kind of tree. It never tries to be anything else. This juniper tree never tried to be an oak. It didn't start out as a pine tree, then change. Even though there are oaks and pines all around here it just kept on being a juniper tree. Jackson maybe you tried so hard to be big that you forgot what type of tree you are."

Jackson sat quietly for a moment. As he let the wisdom sink in, he suddenly realized that he was ignoring the man who had served it to him. He turned to offer up a smile and a thank you to Willis, but found him gone, just as quietly as he had come.

As the group left the world's largest juniper tree Jackson helped Steven put his pack on, Steven handed Davis one of his extra snacks and Saffron counted heads.

"All heads accounted for sir!"

"Thank you Saffron."

It was much later in the day than Paul had hoped. Although the group had traveled very fast and covered ground at a pace that was annihilating Taylor, the two hour delay at the trailhead had really put them behind. This stretch of trail was a great place to make up that time. The wide open downhill trail led the group through a small indention in the ground. It looked like a small crater, with celestial origins and a layer of grass growing in it.

"Did a comet hit here or something?" Steven asked

"Comets don't hit, meteors hit." Paul led the group, so no one could see his eyes roll. "But that is not what this is anyway. This is the old pond" Paul explained slowly in order to allow the group to climb out of the other side "that held the water, for the ranch house, here at Reavis Ranch."

They had made it!

As the group cheered they looked around at the pleasant little valley below them. It was a mixture of man's labor and God's love, poured onto the valley floor. There were remnants of corrals and farm implements boxed into a beautiful valley. The tall green grass tickled the bottom of the overgrown apple trees which, like the farming tools and corrals, were evidence of a man's life work, in a small piece of paradise. The group stood motionless atop the old pond as the words of the poem that Paul had recited were almost audible,

His trees survived the seasons, and he saw them rooted well

In the springtime there were blossoms, in the fall the apples fell

"This place is beautiful!" Leslie's jaw gaped open as she finished the sentence and rotated her head to take it all in.

"That old man hiked a wheel-barrow full of vegetables out of here?" asked Steven

"Yup" answered Paul.

"Man, I thought I was tough." Steven was truly shocked that someone else could do something that he couldn't.

"Mister Paul, could you show us the apple orchard?" Willis asked with the excitement of a child on Christmas morning.

"Well yeah, that's where we're sleeping tonight." Paul's answer brought a new air to the conversation, as the group realized collectively how cold it had gotten. The valley sat at an elevation of 5000', a brisk air about it and a very early sunset behind the huge mountain to its west. It was obvious at this moment that the clients had not planned for any cold weather. Davis asked,

"So how cold does it get here?"

"It should get just below freezing tonight, not much more." Paul said nonchalantly.

As the group began to hurriedly put their small camps together it became clear that not many of them had ever really backpacked before. Many of them were opening the boxes in which their new hiking devices were shipped because they had just bought it. Many struggled reading directions, others put small tents up just in time to have a brief gust of wind blow it over. Taylor lay on his back in the confusion, head on his backpack like a pillow, resting, without unpacking anything.

"Taylor, why aren't you putting your camp together?" asked Leslie who had kept a close eye on him after the switchbacks.

"Oh, it's Taylor!" shouted Saffron for the first time understanding his name.

Taylor smiled, still looking straight up from his resting place. "This is it," he patted his pack.

"Taylor that's just your backpack, what are you going to use for a sleeping bag? It'll be cold tonight."

"As tired as I am, I could sleep through anything." Taylor had grossly underestimated the weather and Leslie knew it. She quickly pulled the fleece liner out of the inside of her own bag while Taylor's eyes were closed and ran it over to him.

"Here," she whispered "use this. My bag gets too hot anyway!"

"You are a wonderful person Leslie." Taylor whispered, as if they were both in on a little secret.

As the night grew darker and colder Paul lit a fire. It was the kind of fire that crackled and popped perfectly, inviting the group to gather around, make their dinner and relax in its warmth for a moment before the cold locked arms with the night. As the group gathered around Paul knew they all owed their comfort to him; the clients knew it as well. The fire was a symbol that Paul was still in charge.

"So, any questions about the trip so far?" Paul tried to steer the conversation towards the gold. On most trips he answered questions like "How much is left?" and "What do we do with it once we get it?" but this time it was different. As Paul reached into his pack to retrieve his "edited" maps he was taken off guard by the next question.

"Why do you do this Mister Paul?" came the question from Willis. As the fire produced a couple of miniature explosions Paul stammered,

"Uh, what do you mean Willis?"

"Well Mister Paul, you could do a lot of things. You're smart, strong and know plenty, so why come out here and search for the Lost Dutchman?"

The pain of his childhood flashed, for a moment in Paul's eyes. It was the first time he remembered anyone taking an interest in him. They were usually too tired, too excited or too greedy to care about anything but themselves. Paul twisted his face in a strange manner as he thought back to why he did what he did. It had been so many years since he escaped to the mountains from the pain of his 12th birthday that he never really saw himself doing anything else.

"You know, I guess it's just who I am."

"So would you say you have found your spot in the world Mister Paul?"

"Yeah, I guess so," With that Willis smiled. He looked at Jackson who

was gazing into the fire, mesmerized as he spoke. "I always wanted to be a teacher." Deep silence followed the weighty statement for a moment.

"Why aren't you one?" asked Willis.

"Because Willis, teachers don't make any money. I thought that I could build a perfect life for my family if I had enough money and now I have the money but life isn't perfect."

"So then why don't you go out and make a lot of money teaching?" The entire group looked confused.

"Teachers don't make much money where I'm from Willis" Jackson stated the belief of most of the group.

"And just where did you hear that, the news or maybe your high school counselor who wasn't making any money himself? Teachers make millions of dollars every year. Maybe you just don't know what a teacher is." If flabbergast was water the group would have been swimming at Willis's opposition to a common belief; all except Taylor who smiled and commented with his eyes closed.

"Jackson, I paid a teacher $35,000 last year and he only worked for me two months. He taught me plenty though."

"Jackson you wanted to teach," said Willis "that doesn't mean you have to work in a school from August till May. All you have to do is show people something they didn't know before they talked to you."

"I don't understand Willis."

"Mister Jackson what do you know that you think people would pay to learn?"

"I don't really know anything but real estate and exercise."

"Yes, two of the most lucrative businesses in the country," Leslie chimed in with a newfound hope for Jackson in her eyes as she began to understand. "You said you made $2.5 million last year; do you think there are people out there who would pay to know how you did it? Or maybe people over 50 would love to know how it is that you stay so fit. Jackson teaching is just sharing knowledge and you have plenty to share. Who knows maybe you can make more teaching than you do in real estate."

"Ever heard of Pat Flynn?" asked Davis shocking the rest of the group. "He built a small website that accidentally replaced his income, now he teaches people how to build those types of websites. He's a great guy, and a millionaire teacher."

"Mister Jackson I know you came out here to find a gold mine. I think you just found it." Willis slowly stood up. "Well these old bones need some sleep."

With that the group all began to retire except for Jackson. He was still staring at the fire only this time the glow in his eyes wasn't the reflection of the flames dancing in the night. It was excitement and ideas running through his mind.

He would be the last one up and only retired to bed after the fire was in its last stage of life and the cold began collecting around him. As he lay in his sleeping bag motionless, his mind raced with ideas. His focus was completely singular until he heard Taylor get out of bed.

He stood up from the fleece liner that Leslie had shared, exposing him to the deeply cold night. He began to shiver and walk simultaneously. After a few short steps he began the necessary preparations of relieving himself with his back turned to the camp.

He had no idea that anyone was still awake.

The last image Jackson had of him before closing his eyes was a violent shaking caused by the cold. Before Jackson could drift off to sleep, he could hear the stream hitting the ground in intermittent bursts due to Taylor's uncontrollable shiver. Jackson almost laughed out loud when he realized that it sounded exactly like a sprinkler watering a lawn.

As the sun shone bright behind the mountain on the east side of the valley, the apple orchard remained shaded. It had been a very cold night and even though the entire group was awake, no one wanted to get up and leave the cozy comforts of bed. Paul however knew that the sooner he got everyone up, the closer he would be to ending yet another con. As he rose he blurted out

"We're burning daylight!"

The moans from the group were audible as were the two small whitetail deer crashing through the trees at Paul's bellowing. They had been grazing down by the small creek which still had ice over the top of it. No one heard the deer leaving, except me.

The group slowly began coming to life in the little valley when Steven asked

"Who's building the fire?"

"No one is building a fire!" shot Paul. Then, re-gaining his self-control, he said, "The Lost Dutchman is a long way off. We need to get moving."

"I figured out how they keep the grass so green up here" Leslie smiled as if she had found a clue to the mine.

"Sprinklers, I heard one go off last night while we were sleeping." With that Jackson's eyes opened widely as he tried hard not to laugh. He looked out of the corner of his eye at Taylor who was doing the same thing, only looking at the ground.

"Saffron, that's crazy. Who would put sprinklers out here?" Paul asked, disgusted.

"Probably you" Saffron chimed in. "It's just like you people to interrupt the balance of nature because you think it isn't good enough."

"Well, you can think what you want but I sure wouldn't go to the trouble of putting in sprinklers. Trust me, there are no sprinklers here. I've been here hundreds of times. . ."

Paul stopped.

Had he just blown his cover? He wasn't sure if he had told them this was his first time here or not. He felt like he was losing control. He looked at each person to see if there was any quizzical looks. Fortunately, there was not.

"Well I know what I heard" said Saffron. "What else sounds like a sprinkler going off in the middle of the night?"

"A really cold, old man, shivering while he goes to the bathroom" Taylors face was as red as the last of the tiny coals in the fire. "I'm sorry Saffron, I thought everyone was asleep."

Steven burst out laughing a half a second before the rest of the group joined in. it was an uncontrollable deep laugh from each member, including Paul and Davis that set a great mood for the rest of the day.

"So, where are we going today Mister Paul?" Willis was completely ready, sitting on a log shortly after the laughter died down.

"Angel Basin. It's a lot lower than here. It won't be nearly as cold at night so, no midnight sprinklers." Paul smiled and laughed. So did I.

Chapter 6

The Stranger

-We're all pilgrims on the same journey – but some pilgrims have better road maps- **Nelson DeMille**

A small twig broke under John's foot as he slowly and carefully crept through the trees. It was the only sound that ripped through the unnerving quiet that enveloped the forest. As he approached the closest tree to him, he could see a dark elbow protruding from the silhouette of the crooked and twisted tree trunk.

He slowly stepped closer to the tree and could hear the breathing of the person on the other side. It was a slow, controlled breathing, that was not natural nor was it quiet. It was loud and angry.

John saw the elbow rise and fall in unison with the inhale and exhale as he took another step closer. This time there was no sound as his foot fell. He was close enough to reach out and touch the elbow now, though he dare not do it. The breathing became heavier and John could not tell if it was growing louder, or if it just seemed that way because he was closer.

John felt the cold shiver of fear originate in his jaw and shoot down his back to his ankles in less than a second. He was cold, though the weather wasn't. He took one more step which landed on one small, dead leaf that made the slightest crackle under his army issued boot.

It seemed so quiet. But, as John flinched at the noise he found himself opening his eyes as soon as they had closed. He saw the elbow gone. Time slowed to a crawl as the breathing behind the tree stopped along with John's.

He reached for his army-issued colt revolver and looked down for a split second to make sure each chamber had a cap on it. As his eyes moved upward in the same motion and direction of his pistol, he saw the grey stone tied to a mesquite handle coming around the tree.

It was one of the smaller tomahawks he had seen, which was one reason it was moving so fast towards his temple. He looked for a target at which to aim his .45 and saw white paint, over dark skin. He heard the beginning of a scream that was a mixture of rage and adrenaline that exploded, sharply inside of John's ears.

The tomahawk moved a few inches closer.

He raised the heavy blued pistol in the direction of the scream and saw the eyes of his attacker. They showed of hate, anger and mistrust. The stone of the tomahawk disappeared out of John's upper, left side peripheral vision and all he could see was the handle coming closer. He felt the heavy pull of his finger on the trigger.

But before the hammer could even make its way off its resting place John saw a bright light enter his field of view. It appeared on the left side as the tomahawk reached its mark on the soft temple of Johns skull. Just as the light began to consume his vision John saw the full face of his killer.

He was an Apache.

"John, wake up," Churga, John's beautiful Pima Indian wife, was almost in tears as she shook John awake. She was firmly holding his arms to maximize her effort. But also to protect herself from any unintentional punches that John made while his mind was taking him through his terrifying ordeal.

"Ugh!" John could hear himself grunt, but he knew that it was the end of a scream that had begun while he and Churga were both sleeping.

"It's OK *cheoj*, you're with me. It was just a dream." Churga's soothing voice relaxed John who was still breathing fast and heavy. She slowly let go of his arms, pulled her long black hair to the left side of her body and moved closer to John.

"I'm so sorry, I..."

"*Cheoj*, don't be sorry. Was it the same dream?" she asked slowly combing John's hair out of his eyes.

"Yes, it was the Apache dream" John wiped the cold sweat from his forehead that had offset the warm desert morning. "I saw some terrible things happen to the Apache warriors. War is very ugly."

"John, there's no Apache that can get you. You are a great warrior and you are even kind to the enemy. Remember the battle at Apache Leap? Those 25 Apaches that you took to court would've been murdered by anyone else, including my father. You make the right choices at the right times. That's why the U.S. army hired you to protect us. They made you chief for a reason."

"Honey, they don't call it chief, I was a," John's words were cut short.

"I don't care what they call it, to me you're the chief!" Churga smiled, showing her unusually white teeth. "You've been a protector to my people, and to the whites. My tribe believes that protectors are special spirits that have powers to help others. All you do is help others *cheoj*. You are a doctor to my people, a fighting man when the Apaches attack and," Churga kissed John sweetly on his cheek "very handsome!"

"I'm not that handsome, you're just used to looking at Pima men!" John teased, kissing Churga and laughing at the same time.

"Ugh, you may be handsome, but your breath stinks!" Churga said, pushing John away playfully. "Go get ready, my family is expecting you at the Sundance tomorrow. In his letter, my father says he has another gift for you."

"Your father has already given me too much. He gave me you and look at how much trouble that gift was!"

"He didn't have a choice! I was going to give you trouble whether he gave me to you or not! Besides, if I am right, this gift is very big. Now, go get rid of the dead animal that crawled in your mouth last night!" Churga smiled pushing John one more time.

John raised himself out of the lavish bed. He brushed his hand across the top of his huge mahogany chest of drawers that matched all of the other furniture in the room. He walked to the window and opened it in a wishful attempt to let in some cool air.

He was a letdown. The temperature in the room did not change at all as he flung open both sides of the window at the same time. But, the beautiful sunrise over the desert mountains made up for the sweltering heat that was to come. As John looked peacefully at the spectacular view, his concentration was broken by a holler.

"Dr. Walker, help us." The Pima woman was waving her one free arm at John as he gazed out the window of his house. He had turned a huge portion of the giant building into a makeshift hospital to give refuge to those who needed medical attention.

In the days of Apache raids on the quaint village, his hospital stayed very busy. But since his last foray with the Apaches at the battle of Apache Leap, the small village had remained somewhat quiet.

That is why John was a little surprised to see the other arm of the woman around a man who could barely walk. He was supporting himself heavily on the woman who had yelled at John and another woman on the other side. She looked like the mirror image of the waving lady.

"Bring him in!" John yelled. As he wheeled in the direction of the armoire door, he was stopped by the image of his lovely wife, Churga, who was standing so close she was almost run over by him in his haste.

He flinched.

She did not.

"Another sick man?" Churga asked.

"Yes, he looks bad." John said lowering his eyes. They both knew what this meant. It meant that Churga would, once again be going alone to be with her family.

It was just one of many times that John would miss an important gathering in the name of his work. It was more than work to John, it was a calling. It was the reason he was put on the earth. It was something that he never could explain to Churga, and she never asked him to.

"You are a protector." Churga smiled as sweetly as she could through her disappointment. "Whatever gift father plans on giving you, I am keeping it."

John reached out and held his beautiful Pima bride close for a few sweet seconds and whispered, "Everything I have is yours anyway. I love you."

"I'll be back in four days, John."

John reached into the armoire for his clothes and began to get dressed. "I thought the trip was for a week?"

"I can't be away from my handsome, smelly breath chief for that long. I will leave right after the Sundance."

John stepped in for one last kiss and said, "My breath only smells that way from your cooking."

Churga slapped John on the belly as he ran out of the room towards the patient.

There was a coffin on the front porch when Churga returned. It was a common practice since John turned half of the house into a hospital. But she never could get used to having a dead person lying just outside her front door.

It certainly wasn't the first thing she wanted to see as she arrived home from the Sundance. John was looking at his hands when he stepped out the front door. As he did his eyes slowly raised and met Churga's.

John smiled at the sight of her sitting up on the carriage handling the team of two horses with ease. Then his eyes widened as he realized he was gazing at her over the top of a coffin. He knew all too well her feelings around having the dead temporarily resting right outside her entry way.

"At least one of you made it, or I would have to carry my bag around that coffin myself."

John nodded at the two Pima men who had built the coffin and they bent down to pick it up. It was obviously occupied as the men struggled under the weight, which added a bit more tension to the

already macabre moment. John was holding a strange object in his hand. It was not something that Churga remembered seeing before, and both of their focus was captured by it. He held it out in front of him with both hands quietly.

"What is that?" Churga asked as she stepped down off the beautiful carriage and began to hitch the team to the ironwood hitching post in the front of the house.

"It's a map," answered John without breaking his hypnotic gaze on the old, supple piece of leather in his hands.

"John, they just carried a dead man off of our porch and you hardly noticed. That must be some map."

"It's not the map so much as the story. Come on," John finally shook off the trance, put his arm around Churga and said, "let's get you settled in. I'll tell you the story."

As the two sat down on the huge plush couch under the giant, open bay windows, Churga wanted to tell her husband all about the trip. She was fresh off the time with her family. She was so excited about the gift that her father, the Pima chief, wanted to give to John for his kindness towards their people.

But she could tell that was a story for another time.

John rarely acted this way. It was as if he were perplexed. Being a man who usually never had a hard time making the right decision, this new confusion piqued the curiosity of Churga. She put aside her own excitement to share in the wonderment of whatever John was about to tell her.

"He looked bad when he got here. I knew he would die just as soon as I looked at him." John's distant gaze took him out of the room with Churga, and into the story that he had just lived. His beautiful wife

was sipping a glass of water when she put her hand on his and said, "I have no idea what you are talking about, sweetheart."

"I'm sorry, let me start over. The morning you left, Kikimi and Ira were bringing that man to me."

"Now I'm with you." Churga smiled.

"He was very sick. He had two wounds in his left arm. They were both very bad. I knew right away what had happened. I have seen hundreds of men shot with arrows. So I cleaned and dressed his wounds and made him as comfortable as I could."

John stopped to think for a moment.

"He was very thirsty but I knew better than to fill him up with water. If a man is that dry and you fill his belly with water it will come back up. So I gave him a half of a glass at a time. He would immediately finish the glass and ask for more. I needed something to occupy the time while I delayed held back his water. The poor fellow was so thirsty that I couldn't just tell him he had to wait, so I started asking him questions."

"Well I hope you asked him who shot him" interjected Churga.

"I did. It was the first thing I asked him. But he didn't tell me, at least not right away. He started with a story. He said that he and his partner were in Mexico and . . ."

"Mexico? He got shot in Mexico? Why did he come all the way here?" Churga asked, frustrated.

"Honey, he didn't get shot in Mexico. I am telling you this the same way I heard it and trust me, it will make sense in the end. So they were in Mexico at a bar. He told me they saved a man's life in the bar. He said there were two men. There was a man with a holy shirt and a man with dark eyes."

John noticed the confusion on Churga's face.

"The man was very sick and wasn't making much sense. I thought maybe the man with the holy shirt was a priest and that the he was wearing his collar during the fight. I was wrong. The sick man told me that the one with the holy shirt tried to kill the one with dark eyes. So they saved the dark-eyed man from the man with the holy shirt. The dark-eyed man gave them a map to a gold mine."

"There it is the root of all evil. You know I learned that from you Christians," Churga smiled as she nudged John.

"Money isn't the root of all evil; it's the love of money that is the root of all evil." John smiled "So the two men followed the map and it lead them to those Salt River Mountains north of us." John pointed out the giant bay window above their heads.

"He told me they found it right away. He said it was the richest gold mine he had ever seen and that he and his partner worked it for a few years. I could hear the fluid beginning to build in his lungs. The man was dying right in front of me. Although he wasn't speaking well, I understood his story to some degree. He told me it was hard work, that he had mined for years and finally he had hit the mother lode. Each time they had the gold assayed it got richer and richer. Then one day, one of the mules destroyed the camp."

"That's why we have horses," Churga said, with her eyebrows up as if to accept the credit for owning horses over mules.

"Anyway," John said, shaking his head at the remark. Churga had made him get rid of his mules a few years earlier. John traded them to Churga's father for twice as many horses. The trade turned out to be a mistake as the horses were all horrible animals. Churga's father however said that the mules were the best animals he had ever owned. Maybe that had something to do with all the gifts John had received from him.

"With the camp destroyed, the partner left for town, to replace what had been ruined. The sick man worked what he could with this partner gone and he expected him back in four days." A slight breeze blew in the window above them.

"On the fifth day he heard something coming up the canyon. Thinking it was his partner, he yelled and turned around only to see two Apaches running their horses at a gallop towards him. That's when he said that he knew the Apaches had already killed his partner. He jumped on a horse and left the mine the fastest way he could."

Churga secretly laughed inside as John began to explain the story in great detail, almost as if he were there. She knew that some of the story was embellished as the sick man could barely talk when he arrived. She liked to listen to John's stories though. He was a good story teller and his wildly animated gestures made the stories even better.

"Just before he topped out on the ridge above his camp he took an arrow in the shoulder," John stood up and slapped his arm, "and one lower, in the arm. He said he rode for what seemed like hours to the last water hole in the desert before the Gila. Then the story began to get very strange."

"It's not strange already?" Churga asked, smiling.

John continued, unmoved. "He said he woke up at the water hole with blood all over him. He said that he looked at his clothes and there were strange, bloody hand-prints all over them." John patted his own chest and belly. "He looked down at his hand and it was bright red from fresh blood. He laughed and said 'I looked ridiculous.' Then he said that he reached to the arrows in his arm and they were gone. He said he must've pulled them out in his delirium."

"Oh no!" Chuga knew that was a mistake.

"The wounds were gaping and nasty now and he knew he had done more damage than good. He said he took one last drink from the tank, because he had left his canteen at the camp. He knew it was a long trip to the Gila River but he wanted to be by water for the night so he headed out. The next thing he remembered was lying on the bed in the hospital."

"Where did Kikimi and Ira find him?" Churga asked.

"They had gone out to the first grove of pinyon trees to the east of here. You know the ones that always drop the nuts first. They were checking to see if the nuts were ready yet, and he was laid out in the middle of the trees. They said it looked like he had collapsed there for the night with no water or food. His horse must've left him long before because there were only one set of tracks. They were his, with drops of blood in them."

The moment was silent. The two were caught up in the ordeal that the man had gone through before he reached the sanctuary of their home. Churga's love and respect for her husband grew even more in that quiet and somber moment. He had built an oasis in the desert for people who would otherwise die lying in the dirt in the unforgiving desert heat. Some were able to recover. But even those who didn't were able to find some comfort in their last moments here on earth.

"He was lucky you are here John," Churga kissed her husband on the cheek. "So?" She pointed at the yellowed leather rolled up in John's hand, questioning its significance.

"Oh, yes well this is the most interesting part." John rushed to her side and sat down, holding the map in front of her. "After I got some water in him and he became a little more coherent, he was answering my questions. I knew that his future didn't look good, so I tried to find out about his next of kin, subtly."

"Oh yeah, you are about as subtle as a punch in the face," Churga rolled her eyes.

"Well, I asked him if he had any friends. He said his closest friend was his partner, who he said the Apaches had killed before they got to him. That's why he didn't make it back from town on time. So I asked about his family. He said they were all either dead or in his home country of Germany, which led me to the obvious question. I asked 'do you know how to reach them?'"

"There it is, the subtleness of a skunk."

John continued "That's when he asked me 'I'm going to die, aren't I?' so I very subtly," John's voice raised along with his eyebrows "told him that these were questions I asked all of my patients. But he didn't believe me. He asked me if he had a small bag with him when he arrived. I pointed to it lying on the floor across the room, and he asked me to get it for him. When I gave it to him, he dumped it out on the bed. He had a strange looking razor from Germany and some other toiletries and this." John held out his hand with the leather in it.

"Churga, it's the map to his mine. He told me that no one else knew about it but his partner, and he's dead. He asked if I would take it if he died, as payment. I told him not to worry about that, but the next day he had pneumonia. He was gone very fast. Churga, this mine is sitting, with no owner waiting for someone to claim it. I have helped countless people, for free out here in this desert, and I think that God is paying me back for all that I have done."

"No one knows but the Apaches." Her statement was a reminder to John of exactly what had happened to the last owner of the mine.

"John you've spent years fighting Apaches when they give us trouble. You ran them out at Apache Leap. You have fought and won, and I think we should leave them alone and enjoy our life together, plus I have a gift from father that changes everything."

That statement broke John's concentration.

"A gift that changes everything about a free gold mine?" John looked puzzled.

"Because of all that you have done for us," Churga started but was interrupted by John

"And the mules." He mused.

"And the because of the mules, my father has given you a truly amazing gift. The coincidence is incredible John. Life has such a way of playing out. You know I have always said . . ."

"Honey, would you care to tell me what the gift is?" John smiled. He put his hand on her back and looked at her out of the corner of his eyes, cocking his head.

"*Cheoj* my father has given us a mine as well! Only this one has no Apaches, no lost map and no question as to who owns it. He had the papers drawn up in Phoenix. It's a silver mine named Vekol."

"I know where it is." Gratefulness took John over. "Your father took me there two months ago and asked me what I knew about it. I told him it looked like a very rich mine, that it could bring the tribe many great changes. I asked him why he brought me to it," a tear rolled down Johns cheek "and he said he wished to give it to the greatest man he had ever known."

"John you deserve this mine, my father knows that if you have it, our people will be better off because of your kindness and generosity. Besides you know how to get there already. Who knows where that other mine is?"

With that John opened a small wooden box with a beautiful silver latch and put the map in it, closing and locking the latch definitively.

"Dr. Walker." The voice from outside the window shocked the two. It was one of the men who had carried the coffin away earlier. "I'm so sorry to interrupt but the man needs a headstone and well, we don't know his name."

"Oh yes, I'm sorry. I've been a bit distracted today. Let's see it's a strange German name . . ." John was talking himself through his own recollection.

"I asked him 'Who are you?' and he said 'I carry the map now.' It didn't make much sense so I asked him 'What's your name?' He closed his eyes, and smiled, I remember that he smiled, which was strange to me then he said 'Veisner.' That's it, Veisner with a V."

"Thank you. A man deserves to be known after he dies," said the man.

"Well at least there's no doubt about his name," John said with confidence

"John, guess what tonight is," Churga interrupted.

"I know. It's a full moon. Do you think I would forget? We've had dinner under every full moon since we were wed. Old Veisner and his map couldn't spoil our date."

"Good because I am so hungry!"

That night the moon shone full and bright. It was the type of moon that doubled in size from the night before. It shone so bright that any object under its reflection cast a shadow on the ground below it. Up on the ridge, above the mine there was a shadow of a man.

His silhouette haunted the edge of the ridge about a mile south of the mine. He was standing over two bodies that were laid out neatly on the precipice above the deep canyon below. Each dead man was wearing traditional Apache clothing, their skin painted as warriors. The leather pants and breastplates were evidence that the men were ready for anything, except for the bullet holes that were driven through the breastplates, deep into their chest.

They were the picture perfect examples of dead, Apache warriors, except for one thing. They each had a mustache. Apaches did not wear mustaches. The killer was squatted over the bodies, examining the mustaches as his own long beard drug over the chest of one of the men. He turned, without standing, to examine the contents of two saddle bags.

He had taken them off of the dead men's horses shortly after killing the men.

He angrily pulled out pistols, a small amount of flour and oil, some pesos and a note in Spanish. He could not understand the entire note but there were a few words that he could make out. "*Muerta*," was death or murder and was written multiple times throughout the letter. In one instance it was compounded with "*deseado*", attempted murder. "*Mina*" meant mine, which must have been a reference to the gold mine. "*Regresar con el oro,*" meant to return with the gold.

Then at the bottom of the page were the words that made the entire letter very clear. It was three words that were not just words but a name, a name that put the picture into a much clearer focus. The very neat signature of Don Miguel Peralta graced the end of the letter in its very sweeping and beautiful form.

Under the letter were the clothes the men were wearing prior to putting on their Apache costumes. Old boots, jeans made by Levi Strauss, that were old and ragged and in one of the bags was a shirt. It had a very interesting quality to it, though it took some time to figure out why.

It was ragged and faded with a few holes scattered about in no particular order. The holes were indistinctive and suggested a shirt worn by a man who had worked hard in it. The holes were unremarkable, all but one.

It was a hole about the size of a shot glass in the upper part of the left sleeve that set the shirt apart. It was the older version of the shirt that was worn by the man who had tried to kill Peralta in the bar years earlier. Jacob recognized it as soon as he saw the hole. He dropped the shirt to his side and looked at the body of the man furthest from the edge of the cliff.

He could see it now.

The images of the man turning, after the slap from Peralta, and the frozen picture of him as he reached his knife high above his head, were burnt into Jacob's mind. He could make out the face, though twisted in death, in the bright light of the huge moon that hung directly over the scene. He glanced at the letter, then at the man before understanding what had happened.

Peralta, in a moment of drunken weakness, had given away the only thing of value he had left in his life. Because he was broke, he had to rely on favors in order to get it back. He had approached the only man left in Mexico who owed him anything, the man who had tried to kill him.

It was *El Tramposo*.

Peralta must have struck a deal with him in order to get his fortune back. Fortunately for Jacob the man was no stronger, wiser, or better than he was years ago in the bar. Jacob had easily run down the men shortly after watching them shoot Weisner in the arm. After catching up to them Waltz easily killed the stranger and mortally wounded *El Tramposo*, though he didn't yet know who he was.

He groaned incessantly. Jacob knew that he would die, but waited hours after the moaning stopped to verify his work. He noticed the mustaches and knew that something was wrong. Had they been Apache, he would have left them there, but knowing they were not, he had to figure out who they were and, more importantly, cover his own tracks.

Jacob did not have the luxury of going after his partner. He knew that the only thing that could save Weisner was the kindness of a stranger, a stranger who may not take kindly to the murder of two Mexicans by a German immigrant.

It took a few days for Jacob to formulate his plan. First, the bodies were carried to the edge of this bluff by their own horses. Jacob took the saddle bags before shooting each horse on the edge and letting the animal fall to the bottom of the canyon below.

He hated that part the most.

He knew the buzzards would get to them before any human, erasing any evidence that pointed to anything but an accident. By the time anyone found them they would be a bleached pile of bones in Apache garb. That was better for Jacob than two Mexicans who were murdered by an immigrant protecting a mine, for which he had no claim.

"You chose the wrong friend," Jacob said as he kicked the unfamiliar body off the edge and watched it fall in the same general direction as the horses.

"Und you chose the wrong enemy." With that Jacob finished the deed and kicked the small, unsuccessful assassin into his final resting place at the bottom of a nameless mountain.

Jacob slowly crawled onto Zicke. He reached into his pocket for a piece of candy and found none there.

"I'm sorry my friend. It seems I have lost your treats in all of the confusion. Ve must head to town und find you some more. Maybe Veisner vill be there," he said, almost trying to comfort the animal. But Jacob headed west towards Phoenix, knowing that only half of his sentence was true.

He could find some candy there, but he would never see Weisner again.

Chapter 7

A Stack of Money

-Walking with a friend in the dark is better than walking alone in the light-
Helen Keller

"Whoa!" Taylor shouted, as he tried to stand on wobbly legs under the weight of his pack. He had noticed his extremely sore muscles the moment he had woken up, but his stubborn Texas pride wouldn't allow him to say anything about it.

As the group was getting ready to leave Reavis Ranch he scanned them, trying to see if he was the only one who was in as much pain. Obviously Paul looked fine but, much like Taylor, probably wouldn't show it if he were not. Davis and Jackson appeared to be functioning well. Saffron had been the second one packed after Willis and was literally chasing butterflies while Steven pretended not to watch her.

Then Taylor saw Leslie. She was stubbornly packing up her camp with her jaw clenched when a tear rolled down her cheek. She looked around to see if anyone had noticed and, missing Taylor's nonchalant glances, she pulled a bottle of medication out of her pack. She took some of its contents very fast, with no water. As she replaced her pill bottle, Taylor quietly approached her. She jumped when he said, "Hurts, don't it?"

"What?" she asked sharply, wiping away tears that weren't there.

"Ain't you sore? You look about ten times better than I feel, and that can't be good!" Taylor ended with a reassuring smile.

"Oh, yeah," Leslie stammered then began to ham it up, rubbing her right thigh "my legs, they're really sore."

Taylor cocked his head sideways, confused. He half-smiled and reached out towards her, "Well, thanks for this." He held out her fleece liner that had been his only protection from the cold of the night.

"Thank you," Leslie looked up and smiled, "not Tyler."

"Why, you're welcome, not Wesley!" The joke broke the tension just in time. At that moment Paul bellowed,

"Two-minute warning!"

"What's that?" asked Saffron dropping her hands as a butterfly flew away from her.

The muscles in Paul's strong jawline bulged as he forced a smile and said, "It means you got two minutes to be ready."

"But, I am ready," Saffron said, a little perturbed that Paul had interrupted her moment with nature.

"Fine, two-minute warning for everyone else!" Paul yelled.

"That's better," Saffron saluted Paul as they both turned. Paul was met immediately by Willis who was smiling. His excitement made Paul smile.

"Mister Paul, it looks like we won't need those two minutes. Everyone is ready." Willis had somehow managed to have most of the group packed up and behind him as he approached Paul. Only Saffron and Leslie were not yet gathered.

"We'd like to have a nice prayer before we leave, care to join us?" Willis turned sideways and slightly raised his arm, gesturing to an open spot within the circle.

"Willis, you're a kind man, but no. It is the Superstition Mountains, I guess you can have your superstition. I'll be over here." Paul walked away as Leslie and Saffron made their way into the group.

The hike out of Reavis Ranch left the group feeling as though they had stepped back in time and were now re-entering the present. As the shaded, green valley slowly gave way to the high desert, Taylor's legs started to loosen up and the group's motion smoothed out. They covered the three miles to Plow Saddle spring in just over an hour. As the trail dipped down into a small ravine, the smell of moss mixed with the sound of water. Steven ran down to the cement tank in the bottom of the ravine yelling, "Water, water!"

"What's his deal?" asked Jackson taking a sip from the tube that came out of his water bladder. He had filled it at the spring at Reavis Ranch along with most of the others.

"I don't think he got water this morning," Leslie answered

"Oh no!" Steven dropped his backpack and fell down to his knees at the tank. "That water sound is just a mirage!"

"Hey nimrod," yelled Taylor "you don't hear a mirage, you see one and that sound is real. Just look at the crick!"

Below the tank ran a beautiful little stream that dropped into a small pool 200 feet down from rectangular tank that Steven was now leaving, along with his pack.

"Mister Paul, who were Bacon and Upton?" asked Willis pointing to the inscription 'Bacon and Upton 12-2-48' on the side of the tank.

"They were real cowboys Willis." Paul smiled as he prepared to tell a story, riddled with lies. "Hoolie Bacon and Charlie Upton were ranchers who owned a lot of this land, including Reavis Ranch."

"I thought Elisha Reavis owned it," Saffron questioned Paul with her hands on her hips.

"He did," Paul closed his eyes tightly, mustering all of what little patience he had, "that is 'til he died, then other people owned it." Paul spoke like he was talking to a child. "Some of those people were John Bacon and Charlie Upton, real cowboys and real friends."

Taylor noticed Davis becoming fidgety at the utterance of the word friends. "Look Davis," Taylor drawled, "I know that Steven comes on a little strong. He just took a shine to you. We don't run into other well drillers much."

"What are you talking about?" Davis questioned as the others glanced, in confusion at each other.

"Well I seen how you got a little nervous when Paul said friends. I just thought it was Steven. He can be, well he is annoying, but he sure seems to like you." Taylor looked a little embarrassed. But he spoke like a man giving a speech that he had given over and over again.

"Oh, no," Davis quickly recanted, "well, I mean, yeah. A little bit of Steven goes a long way, but that's not what I was thinking."

"What were you thinking?" Paul's eyebrows furrowed deeply above his questioning eyes.

"Well, I don't know, it's just that, well," Davis let his voice slowly trail off as he filled the questioning air with meaningless words. Then, the focus of his nervousness came out, almost in a whisper. "I just don't think friends are that important."

Everyone but Steven heard the meek statement. For a moment, there was no motion from the party. All eyes settled on Willis who was looking at the inscription when he asked, "Why not?"

Davis wore his discomfort on his face as he answered, "Trying to make friends is a lot of work and I do just fine on my own."

"Trying to have friends might be the worst way to get them." Willis smiled as he spoke. "Mister Davis have you ever met someone who came on real strong; a person who made people a little uncomfortable when they were around by their behavior, even though they thought everyone liked them?"

Every person turned their head slowly down the creek towards Steven. As he raised his face up out of the water he shook off the excess, pulled back his hair and noticed the attention. Seeing the opportunity he blurted out,

"If ice were water it'd be this water! You know, because it's cold?" Stevens's eyebrows shot up as he asked his last statement hoping that someone would get it. He realized they didn't when they all turned away. Heads nodded in agreement as Steven had proved Willis' point.

"Mister Davis, you can't make someone like you. You can only become likable. You can become happy, funny, smart, kind or any number of things. The person you become is what attracts friends, and for that matter success."

"Willis," Davis said moving his eyes down towards the names in the tank, "I understand but I just don't care. I do fine without friends. I have a good job, I stay pretty healthy, and I take care of business so why would I need to go get friends?"

 "Because you are the average of the people that you spend the most time with." Willis stated as Paul looked right at me.

"What do you mean?" Davis quickly, and for the first time looked Willis in the eye.

"Well people usually do the things that the people around them do. It's not an exact science but there is something to it." Willis sat back and put his hands behind his head, resting against the trunk of a cottonwood tree as if to allow someone else the opportunity to speak, which Jackson did almost instantly.

"It's like Seattle!" Jackson became excited at this chance to teach. Willis smiled and closed his eyes.

"Davis have you ever been to Seattle?" Jackson asked.

"No, I haven't," Davis answered very unsure.

"Davis, Seattle has to be one of the worst places in the country to be homeless. It is cold, and wet and the streets look like they are one huge stone carved out of a steep mountain. I didn't see one soft, flat spot for a homeless person to lay while I was there. And yet, the homeless population is enormous. The economy wasn't bad, but there was a movement of young, healthy people living on the streets in one of the least comfortable places to be homeless. They don't do it out of necessity or because it is a good idea. They do it because everyone else is doing it, because of the influence of everyone else."

Everyone sat, silent for a moment. Suddenly, Steven appeared after his foray in the creek and asked, "Who died?"

Leslie shot him a mean look as Davis said, "No one, were just talking about groups. How a group can cause strange things to happen." Davis carefully avoided using the word friends in front of Steven.

"Oh, you mean like the Atari thing in New Mexico?" Steven asked

"That's the dumbest saying you've come up with," Taylor moaned.

"That's no saying. Atari buried a whole bunch of video games in New Mexico in the '80s when the company died. A few years ago some people decided to dig it up and there were tons of people who came to watch. Computer nerds from all over drove to this dump in the middle of nowhere with their friends to watch some guys dig it up. It was like a movement. Like Woodstock or something. No one organized it or advertised it. They were all just there because everyone else was there."

"Yes, Mister Steven," came the support from Willis as the rest of the group sat astonished "it is like that. The decisions and actions of the group that we are around have a real affect on us. That's why it's important to have good friends. If we try to go it alone we can only be what we already are, but the people we are around can take us to places we never thought we would go, good or bad. Our friends are like a compass for our life."

"So are you saying that if I have friends then I don't have any control over my own life?" Davis asked. "Sounds like a good reason not to have any friends."

"Of course you control your own life," Willis interceded. "Your friends can help to pull you one way or another, but you get to choose your friends. That is the control we have."

"That's why I choose Davis! Front line well-drillers got to stick together!" Steven ran up to Davis, grabbed both of his shoulders and shook him violently, then slapped his left arm and headed towards the backpack he dropped on his way to the creek. Davis looked violated.

Slowly each person recovered from the new point of view they had gotten from Jackson and resumed thinking about the gold mine. They all prepared themselves and, as they collectively headed down the trail towards Angel Basin, Willis asked, "Mister Paul, can you tell us more about the lost treasure?"

"Sure can, after a head count," Paul said without turning around.

"Sir, all heads accounted for sir," hollered Saffron from her position in the very back.

"Thank you Saffron! So you want to hear about lost treasure. Well, we happen to be headed to one of the most famous lost treasure spots in the Superstitions. . . Angel Basin."

"Is that where you found the Lost Dutchman?" Leslie asked excited and strangely relieved.

"Nope, I don't, er didn't even look there." Paul slipped up again. This time he knew they had heard him but wasn't sure if they had caught on. He kept talking as though nothing had happened.

"No, this treasure isn't gold, but it's worth millions."

"Is it guns, or silver from a bank robbery, or maybe a Spanish sword left by explorers?" Taylor could hardly contain his excitement.

"Nope. It's art." As Paul smugly replied to the question, the group behind him looked puzzled.

"What do you know about art?" Saffron asked. The word art coming from Paul's mouth confused her.

"I guess the question is what do you know about art? Ever heard of Ted DeGrazia?" Paul's trademark smile shone through his words, realizing he had the upper hand.

"Yeah," said Saffron "I love the painting 'Los Niño's'. It reminds me that we are all brothers and sisters. The way that the children all are holding hands show that we are all connected. That through the forces of nature . . ."

"He was a tax dodger and a bootlegger." Paul interrupted, not caring to hear what Saffron thought of the forces of nature.

"He was a visionary!" shouted Saffron.

"Maybe, but he came down here to Angel Basin to protest paying taxes." Paul led the group past an Indian ruin on the left side of the trail. It was only an outline of a building where Paul usually liked to stop and lie, but this time the conversation was already in his favor.

"Ted DeGrazia worked the stills at Whiskey springs in the 1920's. That's a fact. He openly said that while he was in college he worked for some characters from Superior, bootlegging in the Superstitions. That's how he got to know these mountains. So in the '70s, when he was having trouble with the courts, he brought some of his paintings up here to Angel Basin. He had a few muleskinners and reporters with him. He burned some of his painting to protest the taxes that he owed. But, they say he hid the rest. Then he died of cancer." Paul shook off the chills that shot down his back as the word conjured up memories of his mother, "He never made it back for the paintings. They're still out here somewhere. Another lost treasure."

Paul knew the routine. If he spoke enough about lost treasure it would keep the clients entertained and mesmerized without offering them many options to grill him about the mine he had promised them. Paul had memorized every ghost story, lost treasure, and death in the mountains for this purpose. The DeGrazia story was one that needed no embellishment to keep the city-ots minds whirling. But this time it was different. This time there was Willis.

"I guess a treasure can be a lot of things." He said looking at Jackson, then Davis. They each smiled understandingly.

As the group meandered slowly towards and into Rogers Canyon none of them knew how close they were getting to where they began the trip. Rogers Trough trailhead, where they started, was named after the same man that Rogers Canyon, where they were now, was named after. But thanks to the forged maps supplied by Paul and the convenient "loss" of Davis' map, no one was the wiser. But there was still one thing with the maps.

"Where is Weavers Needle?" Steven asked, looking at his map and turning it like a steering wheel of a truck.

"It is still ahead of us," Paul gritted his teeth. He knew that if Davis, Willis or one of the girls had asked then it wouldn't come up. But, because Steven was asking, Paul could sense where the next question would lead.

"What kind of name is that? The thing looks huge on the map. How can it be called a needle?"

"It was the best thing they could think of to follow the word Weavers." Paul closed his eyes. He had been through this before and knew exactly where it was headed.

"Why did they have to call it Weavers something?" Davis asked.

"It is named after one of the greatest mountain men ever," Paul was repeating the story he had heard thousands of times, from the woman who had given him his unique name, "Pauline Weaver was the first white man to explore this country. He was an incredible. . . "Paul was not allowed to finish. Stevens's laughter halted the conversation.

"One of the greatest mountain men ever was named Pauline?" Steven could barely speak as he gasped for air. "Sure it wasn't a mountain woman? Oh that's funny, what's that mountain named," Steven pointed ahead, "Shirley's Peak? Oh boy!" Steven was the only one laughing but there was a smirk on the face of Leslie, Jackson and Davis. All three were almost to join the laughter when Paul said, "He is who I am named after."

All smirks disappeared. The moment grew awkward as Steven continued to laugh even harder saying,

"Your name is Pauline? No way, a big fella like you? Oh this is too much!" Taylor punched his son in the arm hard, which slowed the laughing somewhat. The pace of the hike increased dramatically. Each member did their best to keep up with their guide who was hiking at a breakneck speed. None of the group could see Paul's face, wrinkled in anger as he said,

"Yeah, I haven't gone by that name since my twelfth birthday. It's ridiculous." Paul was mostly breathing through his nose now, holding back his anger at Steven. It became almost impossible when Steven said,

"Wow that must have been the best day of your life."

The memory of a ragged old couch where he got the news came flooding back. It had been the best birthday of his life, until he heard one word as the whole family gathered around. The word "cancer" was the last word in a sentence, of which Paul had not heard the beginning. As he looked over to the one person who could comfort him, she refused to look at him, not wanting her boy to see her cry. To most everyone, Sarah Mea Micheals died twelve weeks later. But to Paul she died the night of his twelfth birthday, on a hand-me-down couch, in a company house, avoiding his confused stare.

"Yeah, that was the day I became Paul." He responded with his eyes closed, hiking by memory and feel for quite some time.

To everyone else the day went very well. It was the type of day that felt fluid, calm and steady. Just as the group got tired, they took a break, as soon as they were hungry, they stopped to eat, and right when everyone's legs began to give out, they entered into a canyon that was somewhat of an intersection. It was a place where the canyon that they were in crossed another canyon at almost a perfect 90 degree angle. The grass was knee high in the small clearing where the two trails came together, and Paul leaned against the sign. He wasn't resting, he was covering the lettering that showed Rogers Trough trailhead was only four miles away.

Paul sent the party up the canyon a short ways to a huge cave that was about 100' off the bottom of the canyon floor. Most could see the ancient adobe wall in the smaller cave at the bottom, but inside the bigger cave was a large, two-room ruin that still had the wooden rafters in it. Protected from the weather by the cave, the house instantly took the group back in time. The fingerprints left in the adobe were the first thing that Saffron noticed. As she gathered the group around to look Paul chimed in from below,

"Those fingerprints are over 700 years old you know. The Salado Indians made this ruin around 1300 A.D. and . . ."

"You don't have to read the sign to us." Davis said from behind Paul who was literally reading from another sign that told visitors all about the ruin. Paul had forgotten that Davis was not in the cave yet and had been caught red-handed trying to pass off information as his own when

it was not. "I thought that all sounded familiar," said Leslie who had stopped to read the sign before she crawled into the cave.

As the group slowly spread out around the canyon some stayed in the cave and some headed down to the creek below to soak their feet, rinse off their faces or just to sit and enjoy the evening. Night was falling on the party, but it was apparent that this night would be much more comfortable than the last.

The nice hike had taken them down in elevation 1000 feet, and the temperature was perfect. The Arizona sky was turning mixtures of different colors into sunsets as the night grew. It seemed to change with every passing minute swirling bright purples and blues with fiery oranges and angry reds over the desert where Ted DeGrazia painted, burned and hid his paintings, some with the same brilliant colors.

It was a fitting end to the day and without any prompting from Paul, each person slowly made their way to the flat grassy spot where they had entered the canyon. They each made their camp and settled in. Paul built a small fire. Some used it to heat water for their freeze dried meals, but most just sat or laid in the perfectness of the moment. They were watching the day disappear with a silent pomp and circumstance.

The sun was completely up before Paul had woken up.

As he sat up he saw the whole group was awake. Taylor and Steven were arguing over whose breakfast was better. Jackson and Leslie were packing up with Davis. Saffron was in the Lotus position on a rock halfway between the camp and the cave that housed the Salado ruin and Willis was coming back from a walk. While Paul was shaking the cobwebs out, trying to figure out how to regain control of the group, Jackson, Leslie and Davis approached him.

"Good morning Paul," Jackson said with a strange look on his face.

"Mornin','" grunted Paul, clearing his throat.

"So this morning we noticed something," Leslie said curiously, "when Willis went for his walk, he left some of his things on a rock. I walked past to go potty and . . ."

"Go potty?" Paul asked, with his eyebrows up.

"Yes Paul, girls go potty. Anyway," Leslie was trying to get back to the topic of Willis, "when I walked past his stuff I saw a money clip."

"Oh, thanks for the update, Willis carries a money clip, good to know." Paul said sarcastically getting out of his sleeping bag.

"That's not the thing," Jackson stopped Paul from walking away, "Paul . . . he has at least two grand in his money clip."

Paul stopped immediately.

"Paul, why would anyone bring that kind of money out here; especially him? Look at him, he looks like he's been waiting tables his whole life; cheap clothes, cheap equipment and two thousand dollars in his pocket. Isn't' that strange?" Jackson's fear crept into Paul. What if he was right? Why would the old man have that much money out here, in the middle of nowhere? A better question would be where did he get it?

Paul had made many enemies throughout the years who would have a number of reasons to have Paul followed, arrested, beaten or even killed. In this part of the world, two thousand dollars was enough money to make any of those things happen.

But Willis was such a good guy. He was so kind and generous. Could he be a spy for an enemy, a mole for the cops, or a hired gun for a recent 'client' who was waiting for the right time to push Paul off an edge when no one was looking? The kind and gentle cover made an excellent alibi.

"Oh no," Paul imagined Willis saying to the cops, "I would have never hurt that man."

Then Paul remembered how Willis had entered the group. He was supposed to be on the last trip but a "business meeting" came up. When he called to cancel he told Paul to "take me on the next trip." How did he know there would be a "next trip"? What type of "business meeting" could Willis have? The only possible solution was that he knew it was a scam. He had to.

I could see Paul's paranoia begin to take over. Paul had made a huge mistake letting Willis in the group. He was usually so much more careful. How did he let that one little comment slip past him? Then he realized how, it was greed.

Paul was so greedy that he had become sloppy. He wasn't vetting his customers like he used to. He wasn't checking in on their motives, backgrounds and intentions as he had in the past. He had become one-minded. All he cared about was their money. He had let the cash that Willis gave him cloud his judgment and overtake his common sense.

The moment Willis said "the next trip," Paul should've known that Willis knew. It was a dead giveaway that the kind, gentle old man knew more than he was letting on. The whole trip he seemed to know more about the people in the group than he should have. He must have been studying this trip for months. That was the only explanation. Now Paul was stuck, in the middle of nowhere, with a group of know-nothings and his would be assassin, unless Paul beat Willis to the punch.

Paul had to formulate a plan, but there was one glaring question facing him: Who was with him and who wasn't? It was obvious that Jackson and Leslie were suspicious of Willis; there was no telling what Davis thought but what about the rest? Saffron loved him, and Paul didn't think that the two Texans would stand idly by if something were to happen to him. For that matter, none of the group would stand by if they knew the real story, after all, they had been conned as well. All Willis had to do was tell them the truth and . . .

"Hey, did you even hear me?" Jackson snapped his fingers in front of Paul's eyes to break the trance that he had fallen into. Paul had forgotten about the three clients standing in front of him.

"Yeah, that was a little creepy Paul," Leslie took a step back, "You kind of disappeared for a minute."

"Yeah, uh, sorry it's, well, you know money just makes me think about the mine. Uh, look who cares right? In a few days two thousand dollars will be nothing to all of us. Shoot, we'll all have money clips with more than that in 'em right? Look, thanks for the update, but let's worry about our money, not his."

"Morning, Mister Paul!" The excited salutation from Willis caused three of the four conspirators to jump back. Davis had seen Willis quietly walking up behind Paul, but didn't bother to say anything. Leslie grabbed her chest while Jackson shouted.

"Willis! Oh, buddy you've got to quit sneaking up on us like that. Whew, you scared me a little."

"I just wanted to say good morning, looks like another great day," Willis said slowly turning his head towards Paul.

"Is it?" Paul asked sarcastically, shooting a glare at Willis that caused Leslie to shiver.

"I guess that's up to us now, isn't it Mister Paul?" Willis asked cramming his hand into his front pocket where Davis watched him put his money clip, as he quietly walked up. It was another detail that Davis didn't bother to mention.

Chapter 8

The Debt

*-Friends show their love in times of trouble, not in happiness-***Euripides**

The fine powder that made up the surface of Mojave Street erupted into a small cloud of dust around Zicke's hoofs with every step. Jacob had not ridden far from his small adobe abode just north of a bend in the Salt River. Though the trip had been short, Zicke was dripping with sweat from the heat of the day. Jacob tried not to ride his friend much during the summer. But today he had fed her, saddled her, and nonchalantly started out in the direction of the dusty street.

As he approached Jackson Street, he looked slowly to his right at the quiet, clean home that sat on the corner. It was humble and well-kept with all the typical amenities that a family required. The garden was small but pretty. It was fenced off from the chickens that ran through the almost knee high alfalfa growing in the back. It was not a large field but it was enough to keep the steer from starving and the chickens in a good supply of grasshoppers.

It was the home of Emil and Julia Thomas. Zicke and Jacob crossed Jackson Street. They had not slowed or even looked to see if there were any other travelers coming. There wasn't. Zicke shook her head as they reached the other side of the street and carried on.

"Unt vat is wrong with you? It is a lovely home und I am very happy for them." Jacob defended himself against what he thought the mule was thinking. As they rode past a woman and her small child, Jacob continued the conversation. The child looked up questioningly at his mother as she took a few steps away from the bearded immigrant who was talking to his mule.

"I know she is married. We are just friends. Besides I am an old man, und she is very young und beautiful. She has a vonderful husband" with that Zicke shook her head dramatically almost pulling the reins out of Jacob's hands.

"Okay, he isn't great but he has built a very nice shop for the community und it makes a very good living. It is a vonderful life selling ice cream in the desert all summer long. It beats digging in the dirt und arguing with mules!"

The odd couple crossed Madison Street in the same manner as they had crossed Jackson, unaware. The two rode in a strange silence that should've been normal for a man and a mule but was not for them.

And after the long, slow ride to the next intersection, Zicke turned right under her own direction. She knew exactly where they were going and she picked up the pace.

Jacob looked down Maricopa Street as Zicke took him to where he wanted to go without prompting. It was much busier than Mojave. A small business district lie just a few short blocks away and had a small swarm of people traveling in and out of it. They walked and rode horses or buggies through the dust, conducting only that business which was completely necessary on the scorching hot day. As Zicke's steps increased in speed and distance Jacob slowly spoke of the intent of the trip, though his ride already knew.

"Vell, it is a very hot day und some ice cream would be very nice." Jacob seemed a bit embarrassed and defensive, though he smiled as he spoke.

"Vell I guess there is nothing better to do." Jacob spoke as the abrupt jarring of Zicke's pace began to smooth out into the rocking chair-like motion that he was used to. The pair made the two blocks and the left turn that stood between them and the ice cream parlor in record time. Before they knew it they were on the corner of Central and Washington.

As the distance between them and the E.W. Thomas bakery lessened, the traffic increased. The two were riding through dozens of people now. As they made their way through, most everyone stopped to watch. Every person had reason to gawk at the old man riding by.

Either they didn't know who he was and he made such an interesting sight, or they did know who he was and they had to take the time to watch. It wasn't every day that the source of so many rumors and the butt of so many jokes rode by in person. He captured the attention of the whole street, and though his onlookers had heard and said so many things about him, no one spoke a word.

Jacob and Zicke had turned the small, dusty street into a stage, where Jacob played the hero, or villain depending on the opinion of the viewer. As the small group closed in the wake of Jacobs trail they murmured. There were whispers and nods, pointing and waving and questions and answers, though no one really knew exactly the truth about the old man.

Jacob looked beyond the crowd. He had learned to expect this type of attention, though he did not care much for it. He ignored the giggles and smirks, the smiles and waves and the whispers all the same. He did not care what the people thought anymore. Whether they regarded him as an icon or a vagrant, did not matter.

Jacob knew who he was, and right now, he was a man who wanted ice cream. He wanted the ice cream that came from a beautiful mulatto woman who understood what it was like to be the butt of jokes. She was woman who had adopted a German boy named Rheinhart Petrasch after his family had abandoned him. She was also a woman who spoke German, which made Jacob so comfortable that he told her things he hadn't spoken to anyone else about. She was a woman who had captured the attention and focuses of an old mountain man, and gave him a reason to smile.

The wife of Emil Thomas, she was a woman named Julia.

Jacob dismounted Zicke much faster than usual. He reached into his saddle bags and carefully pulled out a small container of seven eggs with his left hand and a jug of milk with his right. The gifts for the woman were a regular and welcome treat that Jacob had loaded up earlier in the morning. It was a telltale sign that he had started the trip with the destination in mind.

He made his way around Zicke. She was left untied in front of the hitching post on accident. She reached out and nudged Jacob's right elbow, almost spilling the milk.

"Vat has gotten into you?" Jacob asked almost angrily. Zicke nudged the pocket of his shirt that held the sweet candy. It was melting through the wrapper in the summer heat, leaving a small stain on the bottom of his pocket. The stain blended in with the other smaller sweat stains that had barely begun to leak through.

"Okay, my old friend," Jacob said setting the milk on the wooden steps that led into the welcoming door under the sign at the E.W. Thomas Bakery and Confectionary. Jake reached into his pocket and pulled out the two pieces of candy that were causing the stain to grow on his shirt. Looking at the eggs in his left hand, the milk on the step and the candy in his right, he reached out to Zicke and put the two wrapped pieces under her nose saying

"You vill have to unwrap them." With that Zicke took the two pieces, rolled them around in her mouth and spit out one of the wrappers before Jacob could pick up the milk.

A young man standing nearby who had watched the entire scene ran to his mother saying, "Momma that man's mule eats candy! Please, please can I have some?" Zicke looked in his direction and spit out the other wrapper as Jacob rushed through the door.

The emptiness of the store confused Jacob. On a hot day like today he was expecting a line of people waiting for a cold cup of delicious ice cream to calm the sweltering heat. But as he entered the store he found no one--not a single person was visible from the front door. Had

Jacob been a little more careful upon his entrance, he may have noticed that the sign out front read closed. He would have also seen that, even though it was a normal business day during normal business hours, to Julia Thomas the day couldn't have been more abnormal.

"Hello?" Jacob wondered why in the world there wouldn't at least be someone behind the counter.

"Hello?" with that Jacob saw movement on the flour table. As he walked closer he could see that Julia was slumped over, with her head buried between her arms sobbing, each bicep covering an ear, muffling the sound of Jacobs entrance.

Jacob was shocked; he had never seen her this way. He was not sure what to do but he could not leave. The eggs and milk would not make it back to his homestead, and he intended them for Julia anyway. He slowly took a few steps closer and tried to set the perishables on the counter next to Julia. He did not want to disturb her but as he set the care package down something came over him. He reached over and softly placed a hand on Julia's back.

Julia jumped at the unexpected touch. She jerked away and looked up to see the ragged yet clean old man standing next to her. The end of his long beard was resting just inches away from where she had lost her composure.

"Oh Jake, he, he left me Jake!" as she blurted out his name she fell on him, with her arms around his neck sobbing on his shoulder. Jacob looked side to side with just his eyes and slowly and without confidence put his arm around Julia's waist, letting her cry for a long time.

"There, there," Jacob said after realizing that Julia wasn't stopping anytime soon, "calm down und tell me vat has happened."

"Oh Jake, he left me. He took up with that Jezebel and left! I don't know what to do Jake." She had started to pull away from Jacob to tell the story but immediately fell back into his grasp and resumed crying.

Jacob did not have to ask who she was talking about. He knew that Emil had left her. He had seen the glances and noticed the quick touches shared by Emil and the other woman when she was in the store. When she was there, he could feel the tension build between her and Julia. It was easy to conclude who the "Jezebel" was that had stolen Emil away.

Jacob felt no anger towards Emil, though he wanted to. All he could feel was relief that Julia was now rid of the emotional boat anchor that was her husband. He actually felt gratitude that Emil had gotten out of the way. He knew that he could not let on that he was happy. He had to hurt with Julia at this time. He wanted to be her friend, and that meant not taking advantage of the situation. His next question would be an important one, "Did he leave you the business?"

It was the wrong thing to say, though Jake did not know it.

Immediately Julia pulled away from him. She felt betrayed. The first person that she confided in was not interested in her well-being but the state of the business. She answered as she walked to the cash register, wiping away her tears.

"Yes, yes Jake he left the business." Jacob felt the disdain in her voice as she answered his question and sat down in one of the many empty seats at the ice cream counter.

"Mrs. Thomas," Jake said, still referring to her as a married woman, "I know that your heart is broken but you have a very successful business, you are a beautiful voman und you are so smart. This will soon be a story you tell, und nothing more."

Julia stepped behind the cash register, her emotions raced along with her heartbeat. Had Jacob heard the news and barged in unannounced to try to sweep in and steal the only thing she had left? She had heard many stories of the old man. That he was rich, poor, kind, a murderer, hard-working and a thief.

Which one was true?

The man standing in front of her now had always seemed quiet and shy. He had come off very nice, but she could feel that he had ulterior motives when he visited. She always thought that he had feelings for her. But now it seemed that he had appeared out of nowhere at her weakest moment, not to help but to take something that was not his. Julia pulled slightly on the handle of the waist-high drawer under the register.

"Well Jacob," Julia said using his proper name out of anger, "my successful business isn't so successful. Emil took all the money with him. I'm broke." She added a heavy emphasis on the word broke to make sure that he knew she did not have any money. She slowly pulled the drawer open, pretending to punch the buttons on the cash register with her other hand, hiding her real actions. The partially open drawer revealed the butt of a Derringer pistol.

"That is okay, Mrs. Thomas. It vill be a short time before your delicious ice cream vill have you back on top again. There vill be a line of people around the block to come unt buy Mrs. Thomas' ice cream!" Jacob held both hands up over his head and made an arching motion as though he had re-created her sign with only her name out of thin air.

"It isn't that easy. It isn't like digging rocks out of the ground Jacob." Julia opened the drawer all the way exposing the bright, shiny steel of the gun's barrel. This gave her just enough room for her hand and the gun to clear the drawer at the same time. "I have bills. We ordered a new soda fountain from Chicago, and I can't return it. I have a sugar bill and," Julia had tried to be strong but her lip quivered as she finished the sentence "a flour bill."

She was trying hard not to cry, but the overwhelming situation proved no match for her willpower. Tears streamed down her face as she slowly put her hand on the pistol.

"How much do you owe?" Jacob asked the question with his head down, not wanting to see the shame in Julia's eyes when she answered.

"It doesn't matter, no one will lend me the money Jacob, and I'll be lucky if the first white man that finds out doesn't run me out of town and take my business. Who would loan a half-black woman any money? No one Jacob, no one!"

Perhaps the rumors were true, maybe the old man did have piles of gold lying around. Maybe he was a murderer who had stolen a mine by killing the rightful owners and finishing the work they had started. Maybe she would just kill him and take whatever he had. She knew where he lived, and it would not take much to send the German boy over and get whatever the old man was not wise enough to hide. While Riney was gone, she could lure Jacob outside and kill him. She could claim it was self-defense. But, as she had just pointed out, she was a mulatto. Who would believe her?

The horrible situation and the confusion of Jacob's intent brewed Julia to this crazy, uncharacteristic thinking. Her own deceitfulness and anger even confused her, adding to the turmoil within. She felt that the situation would explode at any second.

"How much do you owe Mrs. Thomas?" The stern question came again, only this time Jacob looked at her, melting her defense.

"$2000 all together. Who will give a woman like me $2000?" Julia shook at the mention of the amount. It was a huge amount of money. It was money that she had yesterday before her husband had cleared out everything he could and left. It was money that would cause Julia to lose her composure, self-control and morals. As her hand gripped the pistol tightly, she opened her mouth to call the German boy but was cut short by Jacob.

"I vill." The words nearly knocked Julia over. "I vill give a voman like you $2000 before I would give it to anyone else." Julia loosened her grip on the pistol with one hand and held herself up on the counter with the other. She had not expected this. She could barely stand as the room began to spin.

"Vere is Riney?" Jacob asked referring to her adopted German son.

"Riney, *komm hier*!" Jacob reverted to his natural German, which felt so good coming from his lips. It had been so long since he had been in a room where everyone spoke his native tongue. Part of what he liked so much about Julia was that she understood German, but that was only a very small part.

As the young man entered the room, he smiled at the old German sitting across from his adopted mother. He was tall and slender, and though he did not smile much, he had the countenance of happiness. He was neatly dressed in a white shirt that was pressed, a sharp blue vest that wrapped tightly around his thin torso and a bowtie. It was the same way he had dressed for over a year now as he worked the ice cream counter.

The clean, sharp clothes fit him well, like a businessman. But his long handlebar mustache revealed that he had not totally converted from his roots. His family had taught him early what it meant to be a hard rock miner. After uprooting the family from their homeland, his parents travelled America, going from one boom town to the next, depositing and scattering their children in their haste. So it was nothing new to the boy, who was almost a man, to have someone leave him. Even the disappearance of his adopted father did not have much effect on him.

He did not know about the money troubles and had prepared for this day like any other. He only accepted that the store was closed when Julia had told him, and nothing more. As he felt the tension in the room, he pushed both sides of his mustache into place with one hand and said, "*Guten morgen, Herr Waltz.*"

"Riney, have you finished your chores today?" Jacob asked

"No sir, there is much to do now because..." Riney did not finish the sentence that would remind Julia once again that Emil had left.

"Good boy. Do the vork first, then meet me at my home tonight after you are done. You vill help me bring a package to your mother." Julia let go of the pistol and tried to sit down on the stool behind her. In her dismay she almost missed it and had to catch herself from falling onto the ground. The confusion of the moment kept her silent and had shaken her visibly.

"Now," continued Jacob, "take these eggs und milk and put them away before they spoil. Fix your mother a cup of tea, finish the chores und meet me at my house. Bring your saddlebags und make sure they are empty. Do you understand?"

"Yes sir, but I have one question, must we speak in English?" Though his English was good, Riney was obviously happier speaking German, much the same as Jacob.

The question took Jacob back to his conversation with Weisner in front of the bar in Mexico years ago. He clenched his lips together in a moment of reminiscence then said, "This is America, und in America, the language is English," Jacob said, quoting Weisner.

Jacob turned to walk out the door as Riney carried the milk and eggs back to the cooler. When Jacob opened the door to leave, he heard Julia say something. He could not make out the words and had taken his first step out the door before he could turn around and ask,

"Vat?"

Julia ran across the room to the front door and leapt into Jacob's arms, knocking him back onto the sidewalk. She wrapped her arms around his neck. She was holding her feet off the ground and pulling Jacobs mouth open with the weight of her body on his long beard. As Jacob regained his balance and pulled her up by her small waist, she whispered in his ear

"I'm so sorry." Jacob was confused at the apology and did not know that he had almost been robbed and murdered by the woman he was now holding in an embrace.

"Thank you," she cried, kissing him on the cheek and putting aside her disdain for facial hair. She slowly let go of her grip on the man. But his overwhelming strength kept her from dropping to the ground. After a short moment Jacob gently placed her feet on the ground allowing her to stand and said,

"I vill see you soon, Ms. Thomas" Jacob said, acknowledging that Julia was now single.

"Julia, Jake please call me Julia," came her answer through a tear streaked face and a larger than life smile.

"Julia," Jacob said tipping his hat, cocking his head and bowing slightly. With that Julia turned and walked back into the store, adjusting her dress. Before he could turn around, he heard Zicke whinny from across the street. In his hurry he had forgotten to tie her up. Jacob realized his mistake as he turned to see the spectacle across the street.

The young boy who had watched Jacob give Zicke candy had convinced his mother to buy him a few pieces. He had drawn a crowd as he lured Zicke across the street and threw a piece of candy in the air. Zicke promptly caught, unwrapped and ate it to the cheers of the spectators. Zicke shook her head up and down with the applause, enjoying every minute of the show. However, the cheers came to a stop when Jacob yelled, uncharacteristically,

"Boy!"

To which the entire street fell silent. Jacob took five large steps across the street and was upon the boy in a heartbeat. The boy looked up in fear at the towering image of the muscular old man with his long white beard and sun-beaten face looming over him. Jacob's face broke into a smile that was nearly disguised by the beard and said,

"She prefers the bittersweets!"

With that, Jacob threw the boy a piece of candy, grabbed Zicke's reins, mounted her in one motion and headed out towards his homestead.

It was well past sundown when Riney showed up at the home of Jacob. It was not a hard place to find. But the newly abandoned chores that his step-father had left undone had filled up the day and then some. He was exhausted when he reached the front porch where Jacob was sitting next to his lamp that was attracting a barrage of insects.

"Und vere is your horse, hmm?" Jacob asked

"I walked," said Riney tired and a bit scared of the accusatory question.

"I told you to bring the saddle bags!" Jacob yelled. Then, without a word Riney, who was leaning heavily on the railing of the porch, reached onto his shoulder. He pulled the saddle bags off of his body and held them into the lamp light for Jacob to see.

"Vell, at least you are accurate!" Jacob said with a small laugh. "Put those over here in the corner. You have one last thing to do tonight." As Riney leaned over and dropped the heavy leather bags, his empty hand was met with the handle of a shovel. What little wind was still in him was knocked out by the gesture, and he followed Jacob to a small rock. It was just bigger than a loaf of bread, next to the small adobe structure.

"Move the rock." Jacob said, lighting a pipe and looking straight at Riney at the same time.

Riney looked at Jacob, then at the shovel. Then he dropped the shovel, grabbed the stone in both hands and pulled as hard as he could. The rock did not move. He sheepishly looked up at Jacob as the old man turned his silent focus toward the shovel lying on the ground. Riney slowly let the tension off the rock and hung his head as he leaned over to the shovel, retrieved it and began to dig.

Jacob smoked two full bowls of rich, musky tobacco before Riney had removed enough dirt from around the rock to pull it out of the way. The work was done in silence, not for any reason other than anticipation, on the part of both men, for what lay underneath. Riney grabbed the rock with both hands and pulled for all his skinny little arms were worth. He rolled the rock out of its home in the cold ground.

As he did, Jacob swung his lamp over the hole where the rock once was and revealed to Riney the top of a wooden box. Riney was no longer tired. His excitement had taken over any other emotion when he saw the box top. The old man had told him stories of the gold mine that was now sustaining him in his later years.

Though many people told him not to, Riney believed the old man. Perhaps it was a sense of loyalty to the German heritage that they both shared. Maybe it was that he was the best customer of the ice cream shop; either way it seemed that his old German friend was about to prove the stories true.

"Open the box," came the command from Jacob which was obeyed almost before he could finish. Inside was a worn and weathered piece of cloth. Jacob smiled at its sight, as if it were a relief to know that it was still there. Riney froze, the emotion of his face all drained out as his eyes widened with wonderment. He was in a sort of trance that had taken over his ability to think or speak; all he could do was look. He was shaken back to reality when the old man said

"Vell, it isn't going to jump out! Get it!"

Riney grabbed the cloth in a fist and pulled as he stood up. But the weight of the sack pulled him back into the squat in which he originally sat over the mysterious box. He grabbed a handful of cloth with both hands and pulled for all he was worth. All of his effort barely got the bag out of the box and onto the ground before he let it fall next to the rock.

"It is only 35 pounds! I hope you are tired und not really this veak!" Jacob leaned over, grabbed the bag with one hand and slung it over his shoulder. He turned towards his house with the lamp out in front of him in the other hand dimming the ground around Riney. As the light began to fade into the foreground Riney scrambled to stand. He took a step, tripped over the rock, stepped on the shovel and finally strode out fast enough to catch the old man. Just before they stepped up onto the wooden porch and into the front door, Zicke whinnied.

Jacob sat at his small table that had two chairs at each end. He hung his lamp in the hangar that was strategically placed over the center. The sackcloth made a heavy thud on the table as he dropped it under the light at the same time as Riney sat in the other empty chair.

There was a dark brown twine tied around the top of the bag with which Jacob fumbled; his large fingers awkwardly stumbling over themselves. After a few short minutes he reached under the table and pulled his knife from the sheath on his belt. With a quick flip the string was cut revealing the sharpness of the knife.

As the string fell to the table the cloth opened up revealing a flash of gold that immediately caused Riney to fall into his trance again. He could not help himself. It seemed the gold had a control over him that he had no ability to manage. He had heard the stories, seen people use it to pay for items at the store and even taken some from the old man as payment for ice cream, but this was different.

This was a life changing amount of gold.

It was so heavy and shiny that all Riney could think about was what it was worth. How many shirts, horses or even houses could this small pile of rocks buy? He could not comprehend it. His German family had talked his whole life about finding gold like this, but they had never done it. Now he sat, just inches away from the fortune that had haunted his dreams as a child. This was what the men in his family had worked their hands to the bone to find. They had found no success and now it had found him, through a job at an ice cream shop.

"Vake up!" came the scream from Jacob so loud that it startled the chickens outside.

"You cannot let this silly rock control you Riney. It is dangerous. Many men lose their lives vith that look on their face. It is nothing but a rock. Never forget that!"

Riney shook off the gold fever and told Jacob

"I will go get the saddle bags." He was almost halfway out the door before the old man could stop him.

"No," hollered Jacob. The control that the gold had over Riney was a concern. It wasn't that he didn't trust Riney but he did not want to give him a burden that he could not yet bare.

"No, I vill take this to your mother tomorrow, besides you have too much to do."

"No sir, I did all the chores for tomorrow as well. I don't have much to do tomorrow." Riney almost pleaded with Jacob to take the gold now.

"No, you have no animal to carry the rocks," Jacob avoided the word gold for now, "und besides, I don't mean you have too much to do tomorrow. You have too much to do right now. That rock will not put itself back you know." With that Jacob handed the lamp to Riney and said

"Put the lamp on the table und the shovel on the porch when you are done. Good night." Jacob turned to go to bed as Riney dropped his head, slowly stood up and walked out the door, in the direction of the rock.

Chapter 9

A Growing Storm

-Hope is being able to see that there is light despite all of the darkness-
Desmond Tutu

The pre-trip prayer happened without the usual invitation to Paul from Willis. Something was not right between him and his guide. He felt it best not to push his luck after the cold glare from Paul, though in the prayer he had asked for a special blessing on their leader.

Unfortunately, this leg of the journey had been designed by Paul to completely exhaust everyone on the trail. It was where Paul began to break them down, both mentally and physically in preparation for the huge disappointing crescendo at the end of the trip.

The longest jaunt of the con ended late in the night. Paul had included a small, unnecessary climb for the purpose of camping in a bad position off the trail. During the prayer Paul, plotted about his Willis problem, wondering what to do about the old man. As the bunch headed out of Angel Basin straight south towards Woodbury Cabin Paul, changed everything with three words.

"Willis, head-count!"

Paul had a hard time holding back his anger and animosity towards Willis and it shone through in his voice.

"Mister Paul, there is only three in front of me," Willis said, surprised for the first time on the trip.

"I guess you'll have to get in the back to get a good head count?"

"I guess so, Mister Paul." Saffron shrugged her shoulders as she passed Willis, who had pulled out of the pack and waited for the end of the line to catch up with him. She was just as confused as he was and had grown accustomed to her role as head-counter. But the tone and volume of Paul's voice left no doubt to any of them exactly who he wanted in the back of the line.

Even though Willis had found his new position, he did not yell out the head count. He and I both knew that wasn't what Paul really wanted. The group headed down the trail as a small storm began to grow on the horizon.

"This trail is so easy that a peanut could do it." Steven's new attempt at a saying didn't help ease the tension. In fact, the lack of a comeback by his father added to the awkward silence that was only interrupted by the sound of footsteps falling on decomposed granite.

The line of clients quietly followed Paul step for step until the group had entirely crossed JF trail. That was where Taylor let out a yell, breaking the horrible silence but adding a level of surprise and fear that made the collective feeling worse.

"Get on down!" Taylor yelled at the top of his lungs, scattering everyone but Paul and Steven. Both men turned to find the stocky Texan crouching behind a large creosote bush and motioning at them to take cover. The two slowly walked over to the bush only to have Taylor grab them both and jerk them to the ground out of fear for whatever he had seen.

"Get on down! You'll get your fool heads ripped off! I can't believe it. Hold still!" Taylor was visibly shaken along with Davis.

Saffron was sitting in the lotus position trying to regain her composure with a type of chant that she was performing in a whisper.

"Taylor," Paul furrowed his brow in confusion, "what's gotten into you?"

"Old age," Steven quipped, laughing at his own joke.

"Old age my foot," Taylor's quiet scolding was soaking with irritation, "what's got into me is blasted, man-eating bear, standing right over on that hillside. I think he saw us too. Look Paul you got to kill that thing, before it kills one of us. Hurry Paul shoot it."

Taylor was periodically glancing through the bush and ducking from the sight as he spit out every word in a terrified panic. Steven and Paul slowly looked around the side of the bush to find the source of the horror.

"See the blood dripping from his mouth? Oh, shoot he got someone already. Is everyone still here? Shoot he probably got Davis. Dang it, I was just starting to like that guy. Paul kill that thing before it kills again! It got the taste for human blood Paul, kill it!" Taylor got down on all fours and began to crawl away as he gave his orders of extermination to Paul. Paul looked down at the pitiful sight only to look up at Steven and shake his head when Davis said,

"I'm fine Taylor, I didn't know that I was that hard to get used to, but I'm just fine."

"Oh, dad gum, I meant it in the nicest way Davis." Taylor had crawled behind a nearby rock and was peeking out across the canyon, as everyone's stare turned from him to the object of his panic. In the middle of a patch of prickly pear cactus was in fact a bear, sitting on his haunches, licking his lips with a dark red liquid running out of his mouth and onto his front paws.

"Oh he's got human blood running out of his mouth. Just look at him. He probably drug the poor guy over there when we walked up. Paul kill it! Hurry!" Taylor was close to hyperventilating when Paul screeched at him,

"I won't kill it and it is not a man eater! It's just a little black bear Taylor! Come on man," as he spoke, Paul walked out from behind the bush to get a better look, only to be chirped at by Taylor.

"Get on down Paul! He's got blood running from his mouth! He's got to be a man-eater."

"That's not blood Taylor, its prickly pears! You know those purple fruits on the top of the cactus. If that thing knew we were here she," Paul emphasized the gender of the bear, "would run off as fast as she could. Man she probably couldn't even beat Jackson wrestling. Quit acting like a girl." Paul shook his head and stood up only to be yelled at by Saffron.

"What's that supposed to mean?" She asked, in a huff.

"Well" Paul rolled his eyes trying to think and speak at the same time, "you were scared too weren't you? So if you're a girl and you was scared, and Taylor is scared then he is acting like you, who is a girl." Saffron squinted her eyes at Paul, unsatisfied with his answer.

Paul stood up to the direst of Taylor who was trying to find another position, further away from the bear.

"Get on down Paul, if you won't shoot him at least don't go get ate and leave us out here without a guide."

Paul let out a snort and walked out from around the tree, as he did the bear locked eyes with him in a moment of sheer terror for Taylor. Just as Taylor flinched from the potential carnage, Paul yelled out, "Go on bear!" at the top of his lungs.

Before Paul could finish yelling, the bear stood up, whirled around, slinging deep red slobber across the face of two cactus plants and ran straight away. It happened so fast that Leslie never saw the bear leaving. She was using the moment to take a pill from the generic pill bottle again.

Paul looked at Taylor, who was still crouching behind the bush, as most of the group slowly stood from their own hiding places. Each one was regaining their own composure while acting as though they had not been afraid the entire time.

"Man-eating bear, huh?" Paul sneered, surprised at the tough old Texan cowering behind the bush. "What's next, jackalopes?"

"Yeah," blurted Steven, "everyone knows that jackalopes live up in the high country. The last one I saw was just after we left Reavis Ranch."

Paul turned with an even more surprised look on his face than what he had shown to Steven's father.

"You're joking right?" Paul asked

"No. The last one I saw was on the second day," Steven said with the utmost of confidence.

"Steven, there's no jackalopes. How many times do I have to tell you?" Taylor tried hard to change the subject but with a much quieter, contrite voice than usual.

"Oh here we go! How many times do you plan on having this talk? I know that you're just trying to make me look dumb. No such thing as jackalopes, can you believe this Davis? "Steven slapped Davis on the back, waiting for a reassuring smile that never came.

"Steven, jackalopes are not real," Jackson said, feeling almost sad for Steven.

"Wow, Dad must've got to you too huh? Okay, them ain't real." Steven tried to sound dumber than he actually was which, at this point was becoming very difficult for him to do.

"If jackalopes don't exist, then what did I see when we were deer hunting?" The entire group knew they had become entrapped in the middle of a story to which they did not know the beginning.

"Steven how many times do I have to tell you? Your uncle borrowed that from a taxidermist and set it up as a joke for your mother! Come on son, even she didn't believe that thing was real." Taylor was now pleading, trying to stop the stubbornness of his son as the onlookers stood in amazement that the full-grown man standing in front of them actually thought that rabbits with deer horns existed.

"It was moving, okay?" Steven protested. "Besides I've seen hundreds of them since then. I'm not falling for your stupid joke. You've been trying to make me look dumb for over 20 years now, and I won't let you."

"How, by beating me to it?" Taylor slowly walked away saying "You couldn't melt and pour a brain on that boy." Jackson looked at Davis and shrugged his shoulders in disbelief at the entire situation.

The man-eating bear and jackalope incident had gone completely uninterrupted by Willis and Saffron who were sitting in the trail waiting for the whole thing to end. As the group began to gather themselves Saffron, asked Willis,

"Now why are y'all so quiet today Mister Willis?" She smiled as she revived her faux Southern Belle accent from the beginning of the trip.

"Well, Miss Saffron I have me something on my mind," Willis didn't make eye contact for the first time on the trip; he just sat staring at the ground.

"What is it?" Saffron asked resorting to her normal voice.

"Well, I have a secret. I have a secret, and I think someone has found out about it."

"Can you tell me about it?" Saffron scooted a little closer to the kind old man.

"I'm sorry, but no." For the first time Willis looked troubled.

"So it's a secret secret. Well sir," Saffron brought back the southern charm "your secret secret is very safe with me. I also have a secret secret!"

Willis smiled at her, but it was forced. Saffron's admittance that she had a secret as well had no effect on him. Just then Paul's deep voice echoed off the mountains, "Smell that?" he asked. Before any of the clientele could answer he hollered out

"Smells like daylight burning." With that, he shot a glare at Willis that held him in his place until the group could all line up in front of him. Paul visibly counted each person as if to verify that he did not need Willis, then he turned and headed down the trail.

The group travelled down and around the edge of La Barge Mountain in the shade of the ever growing thunderstorm and in complete silence. Most thought that it was because of the bear/jackalope scene that had just finished playing out, but Willis and Paul knew better.

As the group marched silently down the trail Paul devised a plan. He began to increase his pace. With each step, he gained precious inches on the rest of the group, who were steadily falling behind. As they made their way into the bowl at the bottom of the canyon, Paul was so far ahead of them that all they could see of him was his backpack turning around the next bend in the trail.

The walking flattened out in a beautiful basin southeast of La Barge Mountain, and when each person stepped into the discrete clearing in the trail they stopped. In front of them was a small, well kept cabin in the middle of nowhere. It was not a rustic, run down old home, but a modern house with double pane windows, a nice roof and a stucco finish on the outside. It was the last thing any of them expected to see.

Only there was a problem.

There was no one there to tell them about the cabin. The loud narrations from Paul had vanished, along with him. Each person looked at the other with surprised, questioning looks except Willis, who looked down at the ground. They came to a silent, unanimous decision and without saying a word they slowly made their way towards the home. Then with a shrill voice Saffron screeched,

"There he is!" and pointed to the side of the small barn that stood to the side of the house. She had seen his pack rounding the outside corner of the building and she ran to follow it.

She turned the same corner and stopped.

As she stood in the shadow of the barn, she unnecessarily put her hand over her eyes as if to shield them from the sun that wasn't present in the shade of the building. Then she pointed and ran towards the house yelling,

"His pack!" She had seen Paul's pack close to the house and though I could see that it was lying by itself, from where she stood, she couldn't tell that it had been abandoned. As the clients began to line out in a run, they all ran past the open door in the aged wooden wall of the barn, all except Willis who was still last in line. In a flash, he was abruptly jerked into the shadowy building without a sound. Paul had set the trap perfectly and had sprung it into motion.

Unfortunately there was a flaw. And that flaw was Willis.

As usual Willis had a notion that something was not right. He had prepared for something like this from Paul, and by the time his body was all the way in the shade of the building he had pulled his arms out of his pack, letting it fall to the ground.

When his feet were both planted firmly on the dirt floor of the building, he felt the arm that had jerked him in. He knew it was Paul but could not see anything because his eyes had not yet adjusted to the darkness. This was a small matter because he had done this thousands of times before.

He felt for the strongest part of the forearm and squeezed as hard as he could with his left hand. Then he firmly and sharply hit the tricep muscle above the elbow with his open right hand, also gripping with unbelievable strength. Then he placed both of his feet between the feet of his attacker, turned and squatted as if sitting in an invisible chair that was facing away from Paul. He then stood up and pulled the right arm over his shoulder while throwing his hips upward and followed the momentum with his own body.

His small frame landed heavy and solely on Paul's ribs.

Willis could hear the loud crack from Paul's ribs as his pupil's dilated and allowed him to see Paul's face for the first time. It was twisted in fear, pain and surprise as the puff of dust fell around him, sticking to the sweat drops that were running into his ears creating small rivers of mud.

The entire motion happened in abject silence as neither man wanted anyone to know what was happening. The sound of air escaping from Paul's lungs was the loudest noise in the building and wasn't loud enough to disturb the wild goose chase going on outside. Willis whispered,

"Mister Paul, I'm sorry I had to hurt your ribs. Please don't make me hurt you anymore."

"Who are you?" The conversation started in a whisper that would continue until its completion. Paul thought he would die at the hands of his assassin the second he hit the ground. As the air left his mouth he thought, "That was my last breath. I just died for $2000". Then when Willis said, "Please don't make me hurt you anymore," Paul was astonished. He didn't know what to think, when Willis said,

"You know who I am. I am Willis Washington. Now what in the world is this all about?"

"Why are you here? What are you doing carrying that stack of money around? How do you know everything? How did you throw me?" Paul breathed his questions heavily through a painful voice that allowed his fear to show through for the first time.

"I would rather have this talk in a little more comfortable position, Mister Paul. If I let you up will you calm down?"

"I don't think it matters, you'll just throw me again if I try anything anyway." With that Willis let his knees onto the ground removing his bodyweight from Paul. Both men slowly stood up and brushed themselves off, Paul much slower than Willis.

"Mister Paul, I can answer all of your questions in one sentence. That sentence is, I pay attention."

"That doesn't tell me why you are here." Paul tried to stand up straight but was jerked back to his hunched over position when the pain of his ribs shot through his torso.

"I think it does. Mister Paul I am here because I pay attention. I know what this is to you. This is a way for you to make a living. But have you ever thought about what this is to your clients? This is a last ditch effort at life, a way to escape something or a place to clear their minds. You thought that you were just conning people. Mister Paul, you are giving them hope. Unfortunately, you steal it away from them when it's all over." Willis sat down after speaking and saw the group through a large split in one wall, wandering around the house in circles, looking for the two of them.

"That's what the money is for isn't it? Someone hired you to get even with me for taking their money." There was no longer a reason to lie to Willis.

"Mister Paul, I wouldn't make a good mercenary. I don't even swat flies." Willis smiled showing his very straight, white teeth and causing Paul to relax; coming clean about the trip helped as well.

"What about that karate throw? That was a lot more than swatting flies Willis." Paul cocked his head in suspicion.

"I pay attention Mister Paul. I knew I would never be a big man. I had to learn to defend myself, and by the way, that was not karate, it was judo."

"See, there it is. You know judo, Saffrons name, Jackson's story about Seattle, I mean....how?"

"Mister Paul most people are so worried about themselves that they never stop to look around. It's not hard to learn judo, Miss Saffron has a sticker on her car that says 'My favorite spice is Saffron, just like my name' and after talking to Jackson by the 'World's Largest Juniper Tree. . .'" with this Willis raised his eyebrows at Paul showing the absurdity of Paul's lie about the tree, "I knew he would jump in to teach at the first opportunity. None of these things are hard, if you're paying attention."

"But Willis, what are you doing with a stack of money? They saw your money clip, you paid me in cash. I'm sorry but I didn't take you to be the kind of guy, well, I thought you didn't have, I mean that's a lot...."

"Mister Paul I think you should know something about me. Even if we found the Lost Dutchman's mine, it would not equal a quarter of the money that I have. I won't tell you what companies I am involved in, but I will tell you that you are wearing or using at least three of my products today. I have seen you use over seven of the things that some of my companies make, on this trip."

"Did you say companies, with an 's'?" Paul could hardly speak from the pain and the surprise.

"Yes sir, companies. Mister Paul, I am a very frugal man. I don't believe in debt and I live within my means. Like I told you, I pay attention. When things are cheap I buy, when they are expensive I sell. I always made sure that I was in a position to do either no matter what happened. I have made money many times over just by paying attention."

"I spent my young adulthood building wealth. But it isn't any good if you don't share it, Mister Paul. The best thing we can do with our money is to make the world a better place. Writing six-figure checks to charities doesn't do anything for my soul. Face to face help does." Willis smiled like a man who had found his calling in life.

"I knew that this trip was a scam in the first five minutes that I heard about it. But, I also knew it would be a chance to reach people who were at their wits end, people who are just grasping at straws. That's why I am here, not to take, but to try and give back. In a way you provided me the opportunity to give people exactly what they needed."

Paul was light-headed. He felt as though he had stepped into a mixture between a dream and a nightmare. Being basically thanked for the con by a city-ot who was at the very least a multi-millionaire was the last thing Paul ever thought would happen. It was a rare moment where he was speechless.

"Mister Paul, that money in my clip is for something very special. There is someone with us who will need it badly before the trip is over. If you will pay attention to more than just yourself, you'll know who it is and why."

Willis walked over to Paul and put one hand on the front of his shoulder and the other on his back, close to his spine. Then with a quick simultaneous pull and push he adjusted Paul's ribs. The pop was audible and immediately Paul felt better as he took a large breath in and tried to let the different types of relief soak in.

"Willis about the trip, and this whole thing, I...." Paul could not finish his apology before Willis spoke up.

"Mister Paul, it's been wonderful. Thank you. Now let's go tell the others that I found you, shall we?"

"You won't tell the others will you?"

"Oh no Mister Paul, you will." Willis smiled, stepped out of the door and saw the huge thundercloud building over their heads. Paul took a step towards the door, felt the place where the pain had been before the adjustment and realized that Willis had completely repaired whatever damage had been done to his ribs. Paul shook his head in amazement and stepped out into the open air as Willis shouted.

"I found him!"

The group that was scattered around the house all looked up and saw a much more humble leader walking out the door of the barn.

"We thought you left us Paul," said Taylor walking up and slapping Paul on the back. Paul started to wince, expecting the pain in his ribs to still be there, though it wasn't.

"Wishful thinking," Saffron said, showing her irritation for Paul, though it wasn't returned.

"Where did you go?" asked Leslie.

"He was looking for a place for us to eat lunch." Willis smiled as he covered Paul's tracks.

"Yeah, uh, this is a good spot." Paul was still out of sorts but followed the lead of Willis, though not with much conviction.

As each member of the party found a comfortable place to sit Paul watched them. He saw Davis sit down in front of the barn. Leaning his back against the worn brown and yellow boards he began to get very comfortable, until Steven sat down next to him and interrupted his loneliness. He slapped Davis on the back and pointed at Saffron.

The ever-faithful nature lover was picking her lunch from the shadow of the water tank that sat by the house. She had found a leak in the tank that was soaking a small section of desert floor. Within the wet spot a large patch of bright green watercress was growing.

It took her three handfuls to build a heaping pile which she promptly washed in the water spilling out of the tank and ate.

Taylor, Leslie and Jackson all sat leaning against the water tank, away from Saffron's buffet. Taylor said something that made all three laugh, though Leslie's face twitched in pain as she did. Paul had never taken the time to watch them.

He sat studying them. It was a new experience for Paul to concern himself with the others. His unintentional smile was interrupted when Willis, who had sat down next to Paul without making a sound said, "Feels good, doesn't it, Mister Paul?"

Paul was startled, but smiled as he asked "What do you mean, Mister Willis?"

"Feels good to pay attention, doesn't it Mister Paul?"

"Sure does. It feels good not to have my ribs broken too. So how did you…"

"Mister Paul that storm carries water" Willis said changing the subject. "Will we stay dry tonight?"

Paul looked up at the gathering blackness that was spilling over the bluffs of La Barge Mountain like a waterfall of evil. He had planned for the group to make it to Herman Mountain tonight where he could tell them the story of Herman Petracsh, the brother of Riney, Julia Thomas' adopted son. He could tell them about how the old man spent his whole life out here looking for the mine and had never found it. It was a place that Paul used to let down the expectations of groups in the past but this time he wasn't sure.

He didn't know how much longer he could keep up the con. Coming clean to Willis felt so good. Having Willis sitting next to him eating lunch even after he knew the truth was more than Paul felt he deserved.

He had always imagined the scenario of the first client finding out about the scam and it had always played out very poorly in his mind. It turned out that his expectations were wrong. He wondered what else he was wrong about.

"I hope so," Paul answered the question after the prolonged silence. But as soon as each person had finished lunch Paul started them in the direction of Herman Mountain at a very fast pace.

As they walked faster, the storm grew; as the storm grew they walked faster. Paul was trying to beat the rain even though they were headed towards it rather than away. The trip to Herman Mountain was a long one; typically the longest leg of the journey, but it had always been Paul's intent to wear out the clients towards the end.

He wanted them tired so that their draw to go home was more than the draw of the mine. He had always tried to out walk them on this trail but this time he was doing it for another reason.

For the first time Paul felt some concern for them. This time, Herman Mountain was a safe retreat, rather than a point of deception.

The sun disappeared much too early because of the ever-growing maelstrom that hung over the desert. Paul had led them just over a mile up the 107 trail that led to the Red Tanks Divide when the direct light from the sun was completely gone. As the group began to get out flashlights and headlamps in an effort to see Paul said,

"Turn them off."

"What?" Steven asked, both tired and irritated.

"I said turn them off. That storm cloud had covered up everything in the sky but the moon." With that Paul pointed back and to his right. To the southeast of the group there were clear skies and vibrant full moon that shone huge and bright, facing down the ever-present storm.

"What does that have to do with anything?" Steven's arrogance overshadowed even what the group had come to expect. To the shock of those who were listening the huge man quietly and calmly explained,

"Perspective, Steven when you think that you have the only light, everything outside of it looks dark. But," Paul stopped and snatched the flashlight out of Stevens's hand. He turned it off with a quick flick of his giant thumb and found out quickly that everyone else had already followed his command.

The entire desert darkened quickly and then, in an instant, became a slightly darker shade of bright to each hiker. They could see the outlines of the ridges around them and the brush on either side of the path. They could even see the small trail winding hundreds of yards ahead of them instead of the few feet that were previously lit by the light.

Paul continued, "If you look outside your own light for a minute, things start to clear up."

"Mister Paul, are you saying that our own lights aren't nearly as bright as we think they are?" Willis winked at Paul, who quietly looked down.

"I guess I am Willis."

It was very late when the small party of explorers reached the base of Herman Mountain. Typically Paul would have taken them up to a small finger that ran out to the southeast, tiring them even more. But this time it was different. This time he wanted each of them to feel comfortable. He did not want them to be even as tired as they already were.

Paul stopped the hike at La Barge Number Two Spring and for the first time ever helped each one of them set up their camp before he put together his own. This time he kept them in the nice comfortable flat, where the spring fed a small grassy area so that they didn't have the extra unnecessary hike in the dark up to the higher position where he normally camped.

This time, though they had finished the extra-long hike that Paul had built in to his show, there was a sense of appreciation from the group. There was also content from its leader in letting them camp in the low, flat part of the trail. This time, because of the storm that had stolen the light from them so much earlier in the day, it was the wrong thing to do.

Chapter 10

The Uninvited

-Men are not hanged for stealing horses, but that horses may not be stolen-
George Savile

"It looks like there vill be rain tonight" Jacob spoke very loudly to Zicke. They were miles down the Salt River headed towards the mine. Lightning had struck so many times ahead of them that Jacob had lost count. Though the storm was very impending and ominous, the thunder from it could not be heard. It was the second night of the trip, and Jacob was looking for his normal camping spot.

It had been some time since he had paid off the debt that Emil had abandoned, along with his now ex-wife Julia. The ice cream shop was doing well, and so was Jacob. His relationship with Julia and Riney had somehow completed him. The two filled a void in his soul that the passing of Weisner had opened. He wasn't romantically involved with Julia, but he felt like a young man again when he was around her. She smiled when he walked into the room, laughed at his jokes and understood his German, though he tried not to use it.

"That boy has a lot to learn about mining!" Jacob blurted out of the blue as he smiled to himself thinking about the fortune that he would be able to leave to the young, hard-working man. It was a gift that he had never been given. But now he felt obliged to leave to Riney.

He felt a connection, a comfort and a sense of peace now that he was an integral part of the lives of other people. Julia gave him confidence, Riney gave him purpose, and the mine now had a reason to exist. Before it was just a hole in the ground that the old man used to pay his bills, but now it was an heirloom. It was an insurance policy on Jacob's name. The mine guaranteed that when he was gone there would be a reason for someone to remember him. Unfortunately, at that very moment there was someone trying to rip all of that away. That person was creeping in the shadows behind Jacob as he spoke loudly to his mule.

The slender figure of the man on his horse never fully came into the light. Though he was hundreds of feet away from Jacob, he did his best to remain in the darkness. Following the bearded German in the day had been an easy task. Jacob never made any attempt to hide himself or conceal his path. The man had been sulking from dark shadow to dark shadow since the moment Zicke headed out. It hadn't been hard to keep a small camp a half a mile away from the old man on the first night. Jacob was getting old and so was his mule. The man didn't have to ride very fast to maintain the speed that Jacob was keeping.

Each time he rode close enough to see Jacob, he would hold deathly still until Jacob went around a bluff, behind a tree or down a small draw. The cat and mouse scenario had played out now for two days. It was slow and methodical, like mining gold, or killing a man; both of which the uninvited had planned on doing the next day.

According to the wretched plan, the old man appeared to let his guard down the further he got from civilization, just as suspected. He was much more comfortable out on his own that he ever was in the midst of society. But this time his comfort had made him very vulnerable.

As the man following Jacob slowly planned every step he thought about the best way to finish his task. He knew the area of the Salt River Mountains and hoped that there would be a ledge, cliff or deep ravine that would create an opportunity for this whole thing to look like an accident. He, along with everyone else, did not know exactly where the crazy old German was mining his gold. But because of the secrecy around the mine, he knew that it had to be very secluded, remote and wild.

He was right.

The storm that lay ahead of both men had been a huge asset to the criminal. He assessed that it completely captured whatever attention Jacob had left that he wasn't devoting to his new patchwork family. The distant lightning also lit up the horizon, giving the man the opportunity to get his bearings occasionally. It wasn't hard for the man to make out Four Peaks range ahead and to the left. It was opposite the Salt River from the accidental parade. Horse Mesa made another distinct outline as the lightning flashed directly behind it. The would-be crook was glad to know that they were headed into a region with wich he was somewhat familiar, though he didn't know exactly where the trip would end.

He knew that he would have to follow the crazy German all the way to the mine without being seen or heard. But the ride had turned out to be much more entertaining than he had anticipated. The man, on many occasions, was forced to conceal his laughter when hearing the one-sided conversation that was taking place. A few times he thought the old man had noticed his presence. A click of his horse's hooves, a grunt escaping through a covered mouth when he attempted to hold in his laughter and even the flatulence of his own horse made the hair on the back of his neck stand up.

Each time he would place his hand on his Colt .45 hanging from his belt, waiting for Jacob to turn around. Jacob never did. If he had, the man would have been forced to kill Waltz then and there. That would end any opportunity he might have at finding the mine, but also might make the fight fair. He didn't want a fair fight, or for that matter for the old man to even see his face. After all they knew each other well. The man actually liked Jacob a little. But the lust for gold led his decision to kill a good man for his money. He had let go of the teachings of his youth and forgotten most of who he was, except his name.

Dick Holmes.

Dick stood up in the stirrups of his saddle. He was stretching his neck around the tree he was hiding behind to see if the old man had made it around the next corner. Down the slick, worn leather above each stirrup were the words "U.S. Government" boldly imprinted behind each of Dicks legs. The saddle was exquisite and probably the most valuable thing that he owned. He had gotten it in his service as a government packer. The details of how he was able to keep the saddle, even after he left the employ of the government, had remained a mystery to all but him. Any time he was asked about it he just smiled and answered

"I earned it."

As Dick slowly sat back down in the saddle, convinced that Jacob had moved around the next corner, he adjusted his pistol. That too seemed very official and, though not as beautiful a piece as the saddle, held a value of its own.

It was very used. The right side of the end of the barrel had been worn at an angle that matched the angle worn into the front of the cylinder. Years of being holstered and drawn had chiseled the unique marks into the gun and polished the dark finish to a bright silver.

The body of the revolver was a polished grey; all except the marks on the back. The back of the cylinder and the hammer were a mixture of dark powder burns and rust; a result of much use and little cleaning. Each flash had darkened the exposed metal and allowed the rust to eat small pits into the more damaged areas. Just one look at the weapon gave the impression that it had been used in sinister ways; another detail that Dick had always refused to concede. As he moved the barrel to a more comfortable spot on his leg he whispered,

"Yeah, he's gone."

He immediately shook his head. He couldn't help but think that the craziness of the old man was rubbing off on him. He had never talked to livestock like that before. But there were a lot of things that Dick Holmes had never done before, like become a millionaire.

He had heard the stories of Jacob Waltz just like everyone else in the small community of Phoenix. There were a limited number of rich, eccentric old German men in town. Jacob became the source of many conversations. Dick heard many of the conversations but one thing had made him very curious. It was an interaction he witnessed as he waited for a thin, well dressed Riney Petrasch to finish making his ice cream. Riney was distracted and seemed tired and out of sorts that day. But he perked up the moment that Jacob walked in.

"Very nice job on the rock, Riney," Jacob said as he made his way to the counter next to Dick. "You must've gotten home just in time to do the chores. That is a good boy. Go und fetch her."

As Riney handed Dick his ice cream he wiped his hands on his apron and walked off without getting the payment due. Jacob noticed as he turned his hairy face to the skinny cowboy and grunted his one word greeting.

"Dick."

The heavy accent made the name sound different but Dick knew that the old man was referring to him. As he looked up at the man he could see that Jacob was not looking at him but at the ice cream in his hands. The disdain for the non-payment shone through the old German's eyes and Dick hurriedly reached into his pocket and laid a few coins on the counter before acknowledging the greeting.

"Jake."

Dick looked away before he could make eye contact. He slowly walked to the other side of the room but had no intention of leaving. He had recently left his government packer job to be home with his wife. He wanted to be there when she delivered their son, George Brownie Holmes. Unfortunately for the whole family, his abrupt departure had left them almost penniless.

He skulked around waiting to pick up on some type of information that could possibly end his money problems. He didn't have to wait long. Julia squeezed past Riney through the door that led to the shop. She almost ran to Jacob as his face lit up at her arrival.

"Hello Jacob!" Julia made the exclamation with as little excitement as she could, though most of it seeped through.

"Vy, hello . . . Julia?" He raised his eyebrows as if to make sure that the informal use of her name was still okay. As Julia threw her arms around his neck he surmised that it was.

"I have brought this to you." Jacob tried not to smile but couldn't help himself. From under the bar he produced a sack that he promptly dropped on the bar, with more flair than necessary. The sound of the thud caused Dick to change his position in the room so he could look.

Through the corner of his shifty eyes he saw what Jacob had delivered. They widened as Jacob pulled open the small strings on the pack and revealed a flash of gold from inside the sack. Jacob shot a glance at Dick. He was reminded of the feeling he had when he had produced his wager at the faro table so many years ago. Gold ore always drew attention. Dick promptly turned around and pretended to study the menu on the wall next to the bar.

"This should take care of the little problem we discussed yesterday." Jacob beamed as his attention returned to his philanthropic gesture.

"Jacob, I can't pay you back," Julia knew that he wouldn't ask her too, but it was the right thing to say at the time.

"Julia," Jacob smiled, "you already have. Und besides, there is much more where that came from." Both Julia and Jacob looked quickly at Dick, as if the comment had jarred their memory that he was still there. He quickly walked out the door as the two smiled at each other, not paying any attention to the hypnotic stare that Riney was giving to the sack of gold on the counter.

The sack had haunted Dick's dreams every night from then until now. He could not think of anything but how the gold would take care of his family, how he would never have to work again and how he could manage to get his hands on it. The same thoughts haunted his mind as he slowly prodded his horse into the openness of the canyon where Jacob had previously been.

His mind raced with different emotions about what he would do to the old man. He thought about what he would do with the gold and how much gold it would take to justify what he was about to do. Dick had decided that the comfort of his family was worth this compromise.

After all, he wasn't killing a woman or a child. For that matter he wasn't even killing a young man. Jacob had lived a long and blessed life. He was one of the richest men in town and it wasn't like Dick was taking away much from him. He was so old that he could barely keep his mule up to a respectable pace and when he got off it took him five full minutes to get back on again.

As his horse quietly strode through the soft dirt that lay close to the edge of the canyon wall Dick peeked around the next bush. He could not see through the darkness enough to tell if Jacob was there. He stretched out his thin body again and peered through the darkness, as if the extra couple of inches would make all the difference.

He quietly listened for the distinct German voice to ring out in the usual one-sided conversation the old man had been having with his mule. There were two small flashes of lightning from the distant storm. Then a huge ball of fire lit up the entire sky, as well as the canyon the men were in. Dick quickly sat back down in his saddle, flinching from the light. Suddenly, as if in the place of the thunder that should've followed the electric explosion, Dick heard a sound that was even more frightening. It was the sound of his name, in a thick German accent.

"Dick!"

It was the same sound as the one he has heard at the ice cream store, only much more stern and forceful. He looked towards the voice and another round of huge lighting erupted in the sky far away, bright enough to light up the image of Jacob on the rock above him. Jacob was squatting on his own feet. He was pointing the octagon shaped barrel of his rifle squarely towards and just a few inches away from Dick's top lip.

At that moment, Dick's focus was solely on the end of the rifle stuck in his face.

He could see the round empty blackness of the hollow barrel within the octagon shape of its perimeter. The front sight was very prominent but the rest of the image seemed to fade into the background. Dick's focus grew entirely on the small round opening that could end his life before he would even have the chance to speak. Then, the lightning died and everything went dark.

For a moment Dick thought that the trigger had been pulled and his life was over. He thought that it was almost fitting that Jacob had killed him. At least he had been hunted by a cunning adversary and hadn't slipped on a rock and fallen off a ledge or been buried alive in a mine shaft. He had always wanted to go out with a bang, and he thought it had happened.

Then the darkness faded and slowly the barrel came into view, only this time it was drenched in the cover of the night. It was the same image only deeply shaded and his eyes would not let him see anything but the gun barrel. Then, in a spine chilling moment of terror and truth Dick heard his mistake verbalized in broken English.

"You are trying to kill me, hmm? So vy should I allow you to live?"

Dick realized that if he woke up the next morning it would only be because Jacob Waltz let it happen. He had heard that the old man was a murderer, that he had killed two Apaches in cold blood, and that he would kill to protect the secret of his mine. All Dick could say was, "I'm sorry Jake."

He couldn't lie. It was obvious that he was following Jacob to his mine. With the sidearm he was carrying and the rifle in a scabbard on his government issued saddle there was no mistake, he intended to make the treasure his.

"You vill be much sorrier if I kill you, hmm?"

Jacob touched the end of the rifle to Dicks face. It was cold and caused Dick to jerk away for a moment. But his own movement scared him and he quickly put his face back on the gun barrel, unsure what to do.

"Jacob, I have a family, please don't kill me. You may think I'm a snake. No, I am a snake and deserve to die but Jacob my family relies on me. They need me. Please don't do this to them."

Dick closed his eyes tight and tried not to cry. He knew that he had made his last plea and the next few moments would determine his fate.

"Your family relies on you?" Jacob said disdainfully. "For what, to quit your job, do nothing und eat ice cream all day? I think that you need them more than they need you! I vould be doing them a favor."

Jacob leveled the rifle and held it up to his right eye. Dick shrugged his shoulders and turned away from the rifle, expecting the worst. Then as small pieces of lighting silently ripped across the distant sky Jacob said something.

"But, sadly, even though you are a murderer, I am not."

He pulled the rifle up to his left arm and cradled it, relieving Dick momentarily of the threat of death but making sure the weapon stayed between himself and the quivering pile of blubber below him.

"Jacob, thank you, what can I," Dick's sentence was cut short by Waltz.

"You can do nothing for me. I don't care for you und you are a cancer to those around you. You are a follower, und I have no room for followers." Dick had dismounted his horse and reached his hand up as if to shake Jacob's. The look on Jacob's face was enough to decline the gesture.

"I don't know what to say. Thank you?" Dick asked as he tried to swallow the insult as well as the grace of the bearded man perched on the rock.

"You are not velcome. There are those who chose an easy path, und those who carve out a difficult one." Before Jacob could finish Dick interjected.

"I know, I know. I chose the easy path. You're right. I..." Before Dick could finish Jacob continued

"Unt then there is you, the follower!" Jacob yelled gaining back control of the conversation. "You follow people down the easy path und then try to take what is not yours!"

Dick was shocked. That was not what he expected to come from the mouth of the old man. He had to ask the question.

"This is the easy path?"

"Of course it is," Jacob wrinkled his nose in disgust that the conversation was not yet over, "this is the path that has already been taken! Every path that has already been traveled is easy. Vat is hard is to build your own path. You think that my mine was hard to find, hmm. Vell it wasn't! I went down a road that my friend was building. I followed him. The only difference is that I vas invited!" With that Jacob glared through Dicks eyes in another bought of lightning. Dick felt like the old man was peering into his soul.

Jacob's passion came out in his harsh voice, "My friend was the heart of this mine. It vas his plan und his idea und now he is gone und I am here trying to do the work that we started together," Jacobs accent grew as his anger built, "unt you come along und try to murder me for it! You are taking the easy path from a man who took the easy path behind the man who did the hard vork!" Jacob quickly pointed his rifle back at Dicks face in a fury. He gritted his teeth and squinted his eyes.

He was fighting the urge to shoot off the face of his offender. But suddenly, he realized then what the mine really represented to him.

It was a token of friendship, representing all that he had left of Weisner. He had never realized what it really meant to him. He looked at Dick, whose face was gnarled in fear at the end of his gun. He realized that his act of cowardice had brought out the reality of the mine. Luckily for Dick, Jacob decided that he could not kill the man who had exposed the river of truth about the mine that had flowed through him for so many years. He poked the coward in the face, hard with the barrel causing him to flinch and jerk away. Dick started to cry as he said,

"I'm sorry! Please Jake, I know what I am, please don't kill me, please!" Tears ran from his eyes as he dropped to his knees and held his face in his hands, crying like an infant.

"Killing you won't make you less of a vurm! You vill be dead but still a vurm, crawling around in the afterlife trying to steal from the good spirits around you. I can't send you to your maker as a vurm. Perhaps I teach you, und then send you out!" Jacob hopped down from the rock and pulled the man up by his collar. He said

"First lesson," and with that he slapped Dick across the mouth with an open hand, knocking him down. He smiled as he said, "Never follow me again!" He reached down and pulled Dick back onto his feet. Dick flinched when Jacob let go and said

"Next lesson," then without warning he pushed on Dicks left shoulder blade and kicked his feet out from under him. "Vurms crawl on their bellies. If you get back up then you vill act like a man from now on!"

Dick's breath had blown away the soft dust in which he had landed. His body wasn't hurt but his pride had been badly wounded. He was scared and afraid of the wrath of the old man but also the truth that was coming out of him. His anger began to build and he realized that this was an opportunity for him. He slowly turned onto his side, concealing the holster on his hip. As he got his feet under him he felt for his pistol and found that it was not in the holster.

He looked at Jacob who was glaring intently at him, though he hadn't noticed the move. Then Dick saw his pistol sitting on the rock behind Jacob. He realized that Waltz had taken it during one of the falls. Perhaps he had orchestrated the entire thing but regardless Dick had one last option. He had to stand up and face more of the truth.

Dick stood up.

"Good choice." With that Jacob's voice lowered.

As he patted the dust off of his pants Dick noticed that his rifle was lying on the rock behind Jacob as well. He glanced quickly at the empty scabbard on his horse verifying that he was weaponless. He tried to understand how the old man had taken both of his guns.

"I vill tell you two things," Jacob concentrated on his English, in memory of his friend "Unt then you vill ride back to Phoenix without stopping!"

"Yes sir" was all that Dick could muster.

"First, if you ever vant to be anything in this world you vill have to find your own path. I started working this mine vith my partner. But life had a different idea. I became the sole owner of the mine und my path became finishing vat we had started." Jacob spoke slowly now trying to get more and more of his accent under control. He didn't realize that Dick could've taken his last statement to mean that he had killed his partner. That is exactly how Dick took it.

"That is the first thing. The next thing is this. I vill try to never kill you. I do not vant to face eternity vith that on my conscience. But I vill make sure that you never find this mine Dick. Do you understand? This vill never be your mine. The only vay you will ever have any gold from it is to steal it from me after I am dead!"

Dick's eyes opened wide at the statement. He looked Jacob over and noticed the worn and ragged demeanor of the man holding him hostage. It wouldn't be long before Jacob Waltz would leave this planet and if Dick Holmes could be there, he just might make Jacob's last sentence true.

"Never follow me again Dick. Now get on your horse und ride until you are home. Do not stop!"

With that Dick mounted the government saddle and turned his horse back to the west. He headed towards Phoenix at much faster rate than he had left. The images of the villain grew smaller and smaller as each silent lightning flash marked his progress for Jacob. It took quite some time before Jacob could not see him again. After the abject silence of the long and tense moment Zicke grunted from her hiding place behind a large oak bush. Jacob turned to her and said,

"I am sorry. I vasn't yelling at you."

Zicke repeated the sound and Jacob rolled his eyes and shook his head. He reached into his pocket and pulled out the staple candy that she had waited so patiently and quietly for during the altercation. Jacob placed his shoulder under her chin and scratched her head between her ears as she chewed.

"Vell ve have a lot to do my friend. Ve should rest. After all tomorrow vill be our last trip."

Jacob tossed Dicks pistol and rifle into the river as the thunderstorm in the distance flashed one last rip in the sky.

Chapter 11

A Flood

*-What is the appropriate behavior for a man or a woman in the midst of this world, where each person is clinging to his piece of debris? What's the proper salutation between people as they pass each other in this flood?-***Buddha**

I watched the lightning tear through the clouds just before the thunder woke everyone up. It was incredibly bright against the dark backdrop of the early morning. But the clap of thunder that followed shook the trees around the camp. Saffron sat up in her bedroll. Her eyelids opened so slowly that she was fully upright before they peeled apart. She stammered,

"What was that?" as the rest of the group wriggled to life in the twilight hours of the morning. They hadn't been asleep long thanks to Paul's overzealous portion of the trip the day before. The four hours that had passed between setting up camp and the unwelcomed awakening were not enough for any of them. But it was definitely a problem for Leslie.

She was almost in tears as she rolled to her pack, opened the small pocket on the top and took a number of pills with shaky hands. Most of the group was watching the storm grow around them, Willis was watching the storm that was within Leslie.

"We have to move" Paul said with his eyes closed, repentant. On previous trips he tried to wake clients up early on this day. Typically he needed them to be broken down for the remainder of the trip. But now, disappointment lagged his speech. Unfortunately, Saffron had not heard it.

"What is this, the army? I'm not moving one step until you give me a good reason. Good night."

She finished the sentence as her head crashed against her pillow, just as a silent lightning strike lit up the pre-sunrise dawn. Unfortunately for her, this time Paul was right.

"Your one good reason is right over there." Paul pointed at a small creek that was flowing just feet from them. It was a milky, dirty brown and had debris from trees and shrubs floating on the top of the churning stream.

"Oh, what" exclaimed Saffron "is this the world's muddiest river"? Her sarcasm was felt by everyone.

Paul looked like a man who had been slapped by a woman, deservedly.

He quietly answered, "Flood." Paul never looked away from the current flowing down the canyon, as Saffron asked

"What's that supposed to mean?"

"That's not a river. It wasn't there last night when we stopped or any time I've ever been here before. That's the beginning of a flood and there is nothing we can do but get out of its way."

"Well twist my ears," Steven answered in his usual fashion of confusing ridiculousness, "why don't we just walk next to the flood? That seems pretty easy to figure out." He rolled his eyes and looked at Davis for support. Davis was busy packing his camp.

"I wish we could, Steven," Paul slowly stood from his bed. "We are headed for the narrowest," Paul caught himself and restated, "a very narrow canyon--Upper La Barge Box. If it floods in there, we won' have anywhere to go."

"Oh sure, there's nowhere to climb out or go around huh?" Saffron didn't even open her eyes.

"Miss Saffron," Willis quietly spoke up, "I think that this time Mr. Paul has the right idea. It seems like we should go."

As he spoke, Leslie calmly got herself under control and started to pack without a word. Every eye became focused on her quiet conviction to do what was needed. Without any more comments, the entire party prepared for a long, tiring day, headed into a storm, through a narrow canyon, in a flood.

It took a little longer than usual for everyone to get packed up, but this time, under these circumstances, Paul did not speak up. He stood stoic, looking west at the outline of the narrow canyon, cut into the dark bluff where they would have to start the day. He knew that it would not take much more rain above them to completely flood the small cut. But he had chosen that path for a reason. It was a diversion from the normal path of previous trips. The earlier route would have had him turning north just before the small slit between rocks. But this trip had to continue west, through the narrows. Paul couldn't bear to take the usual route any more.

"Mister Paul, we're all gonna. . ." but before Willis could finish Paul jumped in:

"Just hurry Willis, time is not on our side today." Paul walked off, giving the group time to huddle in prayer. While they prayed Paul looked up, closed his eyes and then, shook his head as if for a moment he had considered his own prayer, but recovered quickly from the thought.

As the group quietly said "Amen," I watched them each begin walking on their own with Saffron and Willis in the back, neither one knowing who should bring up the rear. Rather than argue about it they decided to walk together, tailing the rest.

It did not take long for each hiker to understand Paul's concern. They further they walked the more narrow the gap between the mountains ahead became. Just before they entered into the squeeze of the two mountains, Taylor noticed a fork in the trail that took off to the north and left the watery walkway they were dreading. He asked,

"Can't we take that one Paul?" His drawl was more punctuated this morning from the lack of sleep.

"Nope," came the answer without explanation or reason, though it was a dry and better trail.

Paul walked past the sign that read Hoolie Bacon Trail 111. At that landmark his pace quickened. Though his stride was fueled by a driving need to get out of the narrow canyon before the flood grew too large, he was also escaping a painful memory that had not quite healed yet.

They entered the canyon and the flood water ran from one side to the other. The sound of rushing water grew louder as Saffron said, "I don't think we should go in there."

She was absolutely right, but Paul forged ahead silently, as if she had said nothing. The group entered the canyon with flood water running over the top of their boots.

The water added weight to everyone's shoes, which added discomfort and ultimately more frustration to a day that started with little prospect of going well. The group had walked a quarter of the way through the canyon when Davis turned around and asked Saffron,

"Are we taking any breaks today?" That was all that she needed to vent her frustration to Paul,

"We aren't mountain goats you know."

"Yeah, I know. You aren't fish either. We have to get out of this canyon now. I've seen floods come down places like this in a matter of seconds." As soon as Paul finished Taylor said,

"This water's rising!" Everyone looked at their legs at the same time and noticed that the water had climbed quietly to the middle of their calves. With every step their legs got heavier and heavier. The dirt on the bottom of the canyon floor had turned to a pasty mud that stuck to their shoes and made the hiking even more unstable as they went.

They passed long, beautiful, flowing waterfalls. Each one had a different style and motion with it that made it unique to the rest. Some that fell on rocky outcroppings that broke the water into bouncing droplets, falling like rain. Others rolled down the softer slopes and seemed to grow like a snowball with dirt, weeds and branches from the foliage it was un-earthing.

As the hikers walked past each waterfall, the beauty went unnoticed because with each small stream the level of the water grew. It wasn't long until the water level had reached midway up the bodies of most of the clients.

The bottom of each of their packs were soaked making the difficult hike even more atrocious. While the group continued, the traveling got more and more arduous. With each step they envisioned a wall of frothy, filthy water coming at them with so much power that it ripped trees out of the ground and swallowed them.

No one wanted to be there at that time.

Just as the air of desperation filled the small canyon, Taylor broke the noticeable silence.

"Paul, what is the gold like in the mine?"

Paul could only tell them what he had heard about the gold that Jacob Waltz had mined. There were still pieces of it left in existence that Paul had seen in pictures. Though he had no firsthand knowledge, he described the legendary ore.

"It runs in a huge vein at the bottom of a long steep ridge. Down the canyon from the entrance to the mine a couple hundred feet is a small dugout where Waltz found the end of the vein. He dug it away from view. But inside the mine is the mother lode. It is a wall of quartz that is streaked with thick layers of gold. There is quartz lying on the floor of the shaft riddled with gold that the old man left because it was easier to chunk it out of the wall than to bend over and pick up what was laying on the ground."

The team was enthralled with the story and tried desperately to ignore the water that was rising well above their waists. They plowed on, using the description of the mine as motivation. All but Willis were mesmerized. "They say that 'Ol Jake had a few caches left out there as well." Before Paul could finish Saffron asked,

"What's a cache?"

"Back then" Paul explained, "they would dig out and mine all that they could in the time they were out here. Sometimes the weather, or Indians," Saffron flinched at the word as Paul continued, "or just chores back at home would cut the mining short. So they mined hard until the last day. Then they loaded whatever they could into every spare spot they had."

Leslie sneezed.

"Most times, they had mined more than they could carry. So the only thing they could do was hide it till the next time. So they would dig out a hole or find a cave up under a rock and cover up whatever they couldn't carry out. Those holes are caches. The thing about a cache is that the miner usually had the same routine. So the cache got bigger and bigger and most times they never came and emptied them. So they sit, full of gold mined by someone else, ready to just be picked up and hauled off; unless the Indians got there first."

Saffron had heard enough. In the filthy, belly deep water she exclaimed

"What kind of racist are you? Don't you have any decency? Do you know how rude and hurtful it is to keep calling them that name? You are such a typical redneck."

Saffron's surprising rage was met with nothing but the sloshing of water around the bodies and packs of the group. The few tense moments of silence was broken when Paul quietly said,

"I'm not a racist." For a breath, silence held sway. After a very short moment the sound of water broke through and Paul quietly said,

"I don't call them Indians because it's mean. It doesn't mean anything bad. That is what I have grown up saying. We played cowboys and Indians, not because it was an insult. I don't think the people from India think the word Indian is offensive. Some of my closest friends are what I call Indians. But it isn't just me, that's what they call themselves, too. The word Indian may be offensive to some of them, but none that I know. But I will tell you that the words 'redneck' and 'racist' are meant to be mean. For someone who's worried about labels so much, you sure don't have a problem throwing those words around."

The sound of the water dominated again for a time. The canyon had grown so tall and narrow that the air around them felt as suffocating as the torrent that pushed against their progress. Each person found a way to ignore the miserable circumstances and reflect on the conversation. Then Saffron spoke up almost in tears.

"I'm, I'm sorry Paul. I didn't mean to hurt you."

"Don't apologize Saffron, not to me." Paul stared straight into the water, churning around him.

Saffron asked "Those things I said didn't hurt your feelings?"

"Saffron," Paul spoke a little louder to drown out the sound of the water that had risen to the chest of the hikers, "the only way you could hurt me is if I let you. Some nerds call themselves nerds, some Indians call themselves Indians, and we rednecks" Paul turned and winked at her, "sometimes call ourselves rednecks. If those words describe who we are, then that's fine because we like who we are."

Suddenly the water level dropped dramatically though no one really noticed. They all hung on Saffron's next statement,

"This trip has been a con."

Paul stiffened up, his breathing quickened and his eyes widened. He looked quickly at Willis who was watching Saffron, smiling. As Paul's eyes shifted back and forth in a fit of relief and confusion, Saffron settled him down with her next sentence.

"I didn't come here dig up the mine," Saffron admitted so quietly that Paul would have never heard her if the water hadn't fallen so much. The canyon walls were growing farther and farther apart allowing the torrent and its noise to spread further away from the hikers, just like the relief that Paul felt slipping away.

"I didn't come here to dig up the gold. I came to try and stop you. I thought I could get you to see my way. I thought that I could persuade you to leave nature alone. I'm sorry I lied." Paul's jaw clenched while Saffron quietly cried at her own deception.

Paul found a bank where the group could rest, just as the water had receded to knee high. The sound of damp feet in soaked shoes sloshed through the thuds of wet packs being carelessly dropped to the ground.

Though they had been hiking for a while, it was still early morning because of the surprise start. The air was brisk under the canopy of dark rainclouds and there was a slight breeze. Most of the group felt a small chill but Leslie was shaking violently.

"Steven, Taylor! Help me get firewood quick!" Paul belted out the order as soon as he saw Leslie's condition. Because it had not yet rained at this end of the canyon, there was plenty of dry wood high up on the banks. It didn't take long for the three men to come back with a huge pile of firewood.

Paul put together the small kindling that would grow into the life-saving blaze. It looked like he was doing surgery, making sure that each piece went into the perfect place. Then he pulled an old camera film canister from his shirt pocket. The small plastic tube caused some to smile, remembering the original use of the ancient relic. But Steven looked surprised and asked,

"What kind of pill bottle is that?" No one cared to answer him. But Leslie jumped at the question and felt for her bottle in her pack. It was still there. Paul opened the bottle and produced a cotton ball that was greasy. It was covered in petroleum jelly. He placed the cotton ball below the kindling perfectly. Then he reached into the lower pouch on his pack and pulled out a sealable plastic bag with a box of matches inside. As he pulled out the box, it fell apart in his hand. The seal on the bag had opened in the flood, and the matches were ruined. The hope of the group was trampled. Though each one of them had some type of fire starter of their own, they had all become accustomed to Paul lighting the fire.

Without a word Paul reached into a top portion of his pack and retrieved another bag; this one with a lone lighter and a magnesium stick with steel hanging together on a small rope. Paul had done this enough to know how important it is to keep more than one source of fire in different places on his pack.

The lighter had cracked down one side and the fuel from the reservoir had all leaked out. After looking at the bag for just a moment, Paul knew that he had to use the flint and steel to start this fire. He expertly pulled the devices from the bag and positioned his body between the wind and the would-be fire. He was facing Saffron who was holding Leslie, trying to calm her tremors.

Holding the edge of the steel on the magnesium he quickly and sharply drug the steel across the face of the stick in one motion, throwing hundreds of sparks onto the kindling, but none of them reaching the cotton ball. Paul moved one of the larger sticks out of the way and struck the magnesium again, this time showering the bottom of the fire in glowing sparks.

Almost immediately the cotton ball lit and produced a flame that licked the bottom of the smaller sticks above it, which lit in an instant. The group had a fire and within a few minutes they were each enjoying its heat. Leslie sat closest, warming herself as the rest scattered their most important articles around it, to dry them from the flood they had survived.

As the morning progressed, the storm grew closer and closer. Each person knew that this would be the last moment of comfort they would have for some time so they soaked it in, enjoying the heat of the fire. The hot meal they had prepared and the peace and quiet that surrounded them was comforting.

Paul knew that he had to get them moving but he didn't want to interrupt the moment. The next leg of the journey would be a long one. Suddenly, he jumped from his seat with an idea.

He began throwing some of his extra clothes on the fire, promptly followed by boxes of food and a few other flammables from his pack. "What in the world has gotten into you?" Taylor asked without moving from his comfortable spot next to the fire.

"I'm making room," was all that Paul said. They watched him work. At a fevered pace, he loaded as much dry wood into his pack as possible.

He packed small pieces of dry oak into the voids left in is pack where his personal items had been. Paul began working frantically gathering pieces of grass, small twigs and dryer lint that he had in his pack. He ripped the rope off the magnesium stick and began to bundle it all together. The group sat spellbound as though they were watching a man do exactly what he was put on Earth to do.

He scraped a small coal from the fire with his own spoon and carried it to the pile of tinder on the rock. As soon as he placed the coal on the lint he quickly dropped the spoon and rolled the entire contraption into a bundle He tied it with the rope that he had placed underneath. After frantically twisting, pulling and tying, Paul had a small bundle of tinder, with a coal in the middle, tied into a small package. Then he shocked the group when he placed the bundle into a newly emptied pocket in his pack and forced the zipper shut. As he turned around, all eyes were upon him.

"Paul, are you feeling OK?" Taylor asked, "I don't mean to tell you your business, but ain't it a bad idea to build a fire in your backpack?"

"It's an Indian . . ." Paul looked at Saffron and recanted, ". . . er, Native trick. We need to have dry wood tonight and everything around us will be wet. If we take some fire with us now we won't have to worry about it when we get there."

"Buddy won't that little coal light your grass on fire?" Taylor looked really concerned.

"Not if I rolled it tight enough, if no air can get to it, it should only smolder."

"Should?" Steven asked, taking two steps away from Paul and his portable fire.

"Mister Paul that's a great trick, where did you learn that?" Willis smiled broadly as he spoke.

This was a perfect chance for Paul to lie about his knowledge and experience. It could be an old mountain man trick or even something he just dreamed up. Strangely, he said,

"YouTube. I don't even know if it will work."

To his shock Saffron asked, "You would take a chance like that, for us?" Her new admiration highlighted the question.

"Well, most of you!" Paul laughed and winked. Saffron only smiled and shook her head.

Paul began to put out the fire without the usual command that everyone else get ready. They all knew it was time to go. They were somewhat dry, no longer hungry and fairly content. As I watched Leslie take a few more pills, Paul smiled at her, but this time the arrogance was gone. This time his face had a different look than I had ever seen before, this time he looked happy.

"Leslie, are you okay?" The question surprised her and she turned around quickly, placing the bottle behind her back as she said,

"Yup, never better. Thanks for packing up the fire. That was great." She smiled awkwardly as she changed the subject. Paul just stood there a moment. Then said

"If you need something, let me know." Then he turned around to check on the others. Leslie put the pill bottle back into her pack in a rush.

"Are we all ready?" Paul asked to which everyone mumbled their version of an unconvincing yes. They had all stood up to follow Paul even though they knew they were hiking into the storm that had produced the flood.

The rain hit between Herman Mountain and Music Mountain and it hit hard. Each person had put on some type of rain jacket or poncho, except Taylor who had not prepared well for the trip. As the hike became wetter and wetter, Leslie asked him if he was okay. He just smiled said,

"Yes ma'am I am. Thank you. I ain't melted in the rain yet." He smiled trying to keep up his own morale. Then Steven chimed in,

"It's dryer than a popcorn fart under my poncho, sure glad I brought it."

"I put that poncho in your pack because you didn't bring one!" Taylor looked at Leslie, astonished.

"Well at least I wasn't dumb enough to give away my poncho!" Steven replied. Leslie opened her mouth to yell at him but was cut short when Paul asked,

"Do you two even like each other?" The absence of an answer prompted Paul to continue "You guys are on a once-in-a-lifetime trip and all you have done is argue and cut each other down. Why did you even come out here together?

"That's just how we talk. Sometimes the family just gets on each other. We are still family." Taylor tried to reassure the relationship but the strain in his voice was hard to hide.

"You just get used to each other. When you work with family and live by family they are just there every day, day-in and day-out it's the same old routine. Sometimes you got to spice it up a little." Steven said, trying to justify his insults. He continued,

"Sometimes having family around gets a little boring."

"Sometimes having family around gets boring?" Paul asked indignantly "I think you forgot a pretty important. Maybe family gets boring sometimes but everyone dies every time. One day one of you will be gone and then you'll wish they were here, boring you!" Paul raised the volume in his voice the more he spoke. It was obvious that he was irritated with Steven. "Of all the dumb things you have said on this trip…" Paul was cut short by Steven.

"I know people die, but we still got a long time left man. Calm down a little." As Steven spoke, the group rounded a corner and could see the towering shape of Tortilla Mountain to the east of them. In this setting, with the tension of the conversation and the rain that was falling more and more, the mountain rose ominous in the background. Paul looked at the rock that was perched on top somewhat hanging over the edge of the 1500' chasm below. Paul's face flexed in anger and he said,

"You don't know how long you have left," he dropped his head, "you could die out here."

"Paul, with you as our guide, nothing will happen to us." Taylor belted out in an uncomfortable laugh.

"On my last trip out here someone died, okay?!!" Paul screamed in frustration. He turned around and held his left arm out, pointing towards the rock perched precariously on the top of Tortilla Mountain.

"We were up there. It shouldn't have happened but it did!" Paul slowly lowered his arm and his voice. The mixture of the pain and the truth was violent inside his mind.

"What do you mean 'on your last trip out here'? I thought you found the mine alone last time." Davis pointed out the obvious question that everyone had in their minds. Paul quickly replied,

"There was another trip, alright? Willis was supposed to come with us, but for some reason he couldn't. It was like he knew there would be another one. We were all up on that rock and everyone slipped. Everyone was falling and catching themselves on the person next to them." Paul began to breathe heavily and his jaw was shaking. He looked straight at me for the second time in the trip. "It was like a chain reaction until the last man in the chain slipped." Paul hung his head and bawled. It was loud and deep and was a cry that only could come from a man of his stature. It took a few minutes but he gathered himself enough to finish the story.

"I caught him by his wrist and the straps on his pack, but he almost pulled me off the rock with him. It seemed like forever but it was only a few seconds. We were slipping, we were falling together and then," Paul stopped as if the pain of the memory wouldn't let him continue.

After the prolonged silence he said, "The straps broke! He pulled through my other hand and there was nothing I could do!" Paul completely broke down. He stumbled to a rock and sat down putting his face in his hands which muffled the deep, uncontrollable cry, coming from the huge mountain of a man.

It took a long time for the group to come to grips with what Paul was saying. No one completely understood what was going on.

As the guide was slowly controlling his breathing and recovering from the outburst, Willis asked one question that was not on the mind of any of the other clients. In fact it was a question that was quite out of place. But, as usual the answer to the question would change everything once again.

Willis slowly walked over to the heap of a man piled up on the rock, placed his hand on Paul's shoulder and asked

"Who was it that fell, Mister Paul?"

Chapter 12

The Beginning

*-Time moves in one direction, memory in another-***William Gibson**

Jacob woke up early as usual, but today his time at the mine would be measured in hours and minutes, rather than years or months.

Despite the events of the previous long night, Jacob could hardly sleep. The sun was not up when he started working his mine for, what he knew would be the last time in his life. He grabbed his pick and held it up, close to his eyes. The light of the campfire still flickered from the night before. It lit up the old, worn, rusty head. It had seen many years of digging. Though each side of it was shaped different when he bought it, the relentless picking at the earth had worn the ends into a shape that matched each other perfectly. Zicke grunted at him as he headed past her, towards the opening to the mine.

"Don't you start vith me! I vill vork this hole in the ground as long as I feel like it!" He dropped the pick, and reached into his pocket. He threw a piece of candy at her, smiling at the new twist in the old ritual that the young boy had taught her in front of Julia's store. Even though it was still dark, Zicke caught it. She blew air out of her nose as she removed the wrapper in her mouth and spit it out.

"I don't care that there is ore in the cache!" Jacob justified his actions to himself by yelling at Zicke. "Vy must you vorry about such details? Does it matter to you if your packs are full of old ore or new, hmm? You vouldn't know the difference! I could fill the packs vith manure und you vouldn't care. Have your stupid candy und leave me alone." Jacob retrieved his pick and a small rock lying next to it. He headed to an undersized opening at the base of a long ridge that ran straight north and south. The opening was coincidentally, about the size of the door from the bar in Mexico.

He was carrying a bag and a small branch he had taken from the fire that was aglow on one end. He used it to light the lantern that was hanging on a branch of an oak tree, just outside the entrance. It was one more thing that he knew he would do for the last time.

The lantern light swayed back and forth as Jacob walked into the mountain side. Decades or even centuries of mining had chiseled the tunnel deep. As the miners before him had done, Jacob had followed the vein of gold that ran through a swath of quartz. The path of the golden quartz had twisted and turned with hardly any reason and caused the tunnel to have many coves. The coves were extra diggings where miners thought the gold had played out, only to find the vein had turned and continued in a different direction, getting richer and richer as it went.

It was in one of these dead-ends where Jacob could see two small red dots moving from side to side, about two feet above the floor of the tunnel and just outside of his light. The flash of color caused him to stop suddenly and jerk away. He instantly hurled the small rock into the darkness and stepped to his right. Even his most surprised yell sounded very commanding as he hollered

"Ha!"

The rock made a thud as it crashed into the spot between the red dots. In less than a rapid heartbeat the two red dots appeared as eyes in the light. A large javelina popped his jaws twice and ran past Jacob, kicking up the dust that lay between them. Jacob picked up another rock off the ground below him and said

"I vas expecting a snake."

Jacob shone his lantern light on the walls next to him. There were strange markings that he looked at every time he passed them. They were carved a lifetime ago when the mine was in its infancy. In the wall were shapes that resembled a cross with a hoop on the top of it. There was another that looked like a sun with strange symbols in the middle. Jacob did not recognize them to be English, German or the limited Spanish that he knew. Next to the sun there was a number: 1697. Jacob had always figured it to be a year but wasn't sure. He also didn't care much. Only enough to stop and glance for a moment. This time he stayed a bit longer, making sure that he had committed the symbols to memory exactly and with great detail. He slowly turned away and darkness covered the ancient signs of the previous owner.

Jacob continued down the long narrow tunnel, past the old beams that had supported the walls and roof of the mine for hundreds of years. He also passed the new ones that he had cut and put in. They were made from different types of wood, some oak and some mesquite. Jacob had found an enormous grove of ancient mesquite and had hewn massive timbers to shore up the mine. It had been an arduous process but the peace of mind that they provided him were well worth the work.

As Jacob rounded the next corner he heard the snake before he saw it. The sound of the rattles shaking were a common welcome back greeting that he had become used to hearing. Waving the lantern from side to side he said

"Vere are you? I knew you vould be here."

Then he saw a flash on the ground at the left edge of his light. He turned to face the snake as it was leaving towards the entrance. Jacob put the small rock in his pocket, knowing that the snake wouldn't make the trip all the way out and that he would have to deal with him one last time when he left.

Jacob headed towards the back of the mine. He was in the portion of the mine that he and Weisner had mined so many years ago. He put his pick up to one of the marks on the wall. It fit the thin groove perfectly but was much smaller due to the wear of the tool. The mark was long and deep as though it had produced a huge pile of ore for the men to carry out. Then he looked at another mark. It was much shorter and shaped different. Jacob smiled and shook his head. He knew that

Weisner had made that mark. He ran his finger into the gouge saying, "Ve all leave our marks."

He thought about the work they had done together before the trip to Mexico. He remembered the terrible trip to the tiny bar and the horrible plan to get the map. He could picture his friend; still sitting at a chair that was too small for him at the faro game, watching in horror as Peralta slowly dealt the cards. He remembered how he squabbled with Reavis, and never named his mule.

Jacob usually avoided thinking about the last day he saw his friend but this time he couldn't help it. He had always tried to keep an eye on the other Jake, but he wasn't there when his friend needed him the most. The image of the first arrow into Jake's arm was not as clear as the memory of the second. It was the second one that Jake could not forget. It had sunk so deep that Jacob thought it would rip through the other side. It was in that instant that Weisner reeled and left, and Jacob hollered at the assailants. They focused on him, knowing that because of the distance to any type of help, the first man would die.

Jacob knew it as well.

He wondered how far his friend had made it. For the first time he questioned if he had done the right thing by covering up his own tracks, rather than going after Weisner. But Jacob knew that if anyone had found two dead Mexicans and the mine nearby he would have no recourse, or claim to the only relic he had by which to remember his friend.

He thought about the silly dusty handprint pattern that Jake patted onto his clothes every morning and how even now, every time he gave Zicke candy he thought the phrase 'you look ridiculous'. He wondered what his friend would have been like now. Would they have been able to work the mine together in their old age? Would Weisner have aged better than Jacob?

"Probably not!" Jacob said out loud and smiled.

Jacob walked a few more steps and sat down on a small ledge. He had carved it out a few years earlier as a bench where he could sit and eat lunch. But now it was so far away from the work that he usually either passed it up, or didn't bother to come back to it.

It was still very comfortable. He sat back and looked a few feet to his left and remembered how the wall looked as it stood in that spot the day he made the reprieve. He had decided to undermine a huge chunk of ore that existed at eye level. As he dug underneath of what he thought was the mother lode he found an even bigger deposit! There was a cavity on the floor bearing gold with an outcropping overhead,

also bearing gold. On that day he sat in his makeshift chair and said, "Today I am a rich man, even richer than Peralta."

He wondered about Peralta. He had heard that the scoundrel had come to the U.S. and taken a job somewhere in Nogales. No doubt he had realized that the men he sent after Jacob either succeeded in obtaining the mine and didn't bother coming back, or had failed. Of all the regrets he had about the mine, killing the two men was the biggest.

It was a strange feeling to hate and have compassion for the same man; but that was exactly how he felt for the tiny, would-be assassin. Jacob had wished that the small man would have made better decisions, but realized that he was just a man. He made a poor choice and it cost the life of three men, his friend, himself and Weisner. Jacob wondered for a moment if the men had families. Then he thought about his own makeshift family.

A smile came across the face of the old miner. Covered in dust and hair it was a deep and content thing that grew much too wide, making his eyes squint. The two mismatched pair at the ice cream shop were a strange sight that didn't make much sense together.

A half-black woman who looked young for her age with a full-grown German man as her adopted son made a very odd couple to say the least. But somehow when Jacob stepped into the picture it made perfect sense. For the first time in his life someone needed him and wanted to need him. Weisner needed Jacob but acted like he didn't. Julia made Jacob feel like her entire life, as well as that of Riney, revolved around the presence of the old man.

She made Riney listen to Jacob, though it was unnecessary since he was completely enthralled with the old man. He had been around miners his whole life and never met one who had succeeded. The strange part for Riney was that Jacob still looked and acted the same way that any broke rock hound would look and act. The money hadn't changed him. He was still a miner, which was why he was here in the first place.

Jacob stood up from his thinking chair and headed towards the end of the tunnel. His lantern was lighting the newly formed pathway that had been created by his own hands. It shone on each side of the tunnel at different times as it slowly rocked from side to side with his gate. He noticed the sides of the tunnel getting closer and closer as his pathway grew narrow and short. He wondered to himself if he had become less eager with age or if the vein was slowly playing out.

He looked at the hand holding the lantern out in front of him. It was hard and calloused. His fingers had twisted somewhat with age but they had not slowed him down, much. They were the hands of a worker, someone who had earned their keep and every scar and mark on them told a story. Jacob was glad that he had used his hands to the fullest and knew that he had been given them for a reason; and just a few steps further the reason shone bright in the flickering lantern light.

The wall at the end of the tunnel was a collision of color in the dark cave. The brilliant white quartz held millions of years of heat, pressure and chemicals creating a backdrop that was only upstaged by the prima donna of the show. Huge rivers of gold ran through the symphony of color and melted the image into a glorious confusion.

Though the quartz and gold did not look the same, they fit together in this picture perfectly. Jacob wondered what other beauty hid within the heavy weight of the earth. Jacob stood for a moment, taking it all in. He would be the only man on the planet to ever see this sight, the way it stood at this moment. It was an image that had been worth all of the years of work and labor and an image that few miners and even fewer men would ever see. He smiled again and after a moment of enjoyment, swung his pick deep into the quartz above the shimmering streaks, knocking them to the ground.

It did not take long for Jacob to remove enough ore from the deposit to fill his small bag but still he kept going. He worked for hours chipping away at the best and richest parts of the lode, knocking the pieces to the ground at his feet. In just a few hours Jacob had more ore on the ground than he or Zicke could possibly carry.

Still Jacob continued.

He worked as if he was the best miner on earth and this was the last chance he would ever have to do it. If the reason for living were to mine gold the Lord would have made Jacob Waltz first. With amazing speed and precision he knocked only the best pieces off of the wall of the mine. Then he sorted them with his feet, kicking the richer pieces to his right and those of lesser value to his left. After a short time he had two large piles on either side of him, but he still went on.

Time evaporated around him as he chiseled the center of the mountain into rubble. His feet were covered in a fortune of dust before he finally swung his pick one last time, knocking a huge piece of gold laden quartz to the ground. When the stone hit the ground all time stopped.

The silence swallowed the dusty old man.

Jacob bent down and, dropping his pick, he retrieved the huge piece of ore. It shimmered in the lantern light. The rock contained more gold than it did quartz and was so heavy with riches that Jacob, as strong as he was, had to use two hands to hold it.

He looked at the bag next to his pick and saw the obvious lack of room. He would have to remove at least a quarter of the ore in the bag in order to take this one piece with him and it would be well worth it. But then Jacob did something strange. He dropped the piece next to his pick between the two piles he had created with his feet. It was a perfect picture of the life of a miner, framed beautifully by the stacks of wealthy rubble. Jacob looked at it for a moment, then said quietly, "For Riney."

Jacob picked up his bag of ore in one hand and the lantern in the other. He slowly turned towards the entrance taking a few steps in the direction of light and fresh air. Then he stopped and turned back. He looked at the lode that lay on the ground, waiting to be picked up. He couldn't stand the thoughts of just anyone stumbling into the mine and taking off of the ground what so many men had died earning. He had two caches outside that were full with decent ore but what lay inside the mine was for Riney.

He decided to set the trap.

Jacob hurried to the entrance of the mine with his lantern in one hand and the sack of ore in the other. His pace was so fast that by the time he noticed the familiar sound of the rattlesnake buzzing to his left, he was already two paces past it. He blew the lantern out dozens of feet before he reached the outside and when he finally did arrive into the sunshine he could tell that it was well past noon. He had to hurry.

Zicke flinched when Jacob hustled up to her side and grabbed the saddle bag. She had been almost asleep when he jerked the saw from the worn leather pouch and put the bag of ore in its place with one motion. She arched her neck, watching Jacob and waiting for the ritual piece of candy that never came.

Jacob knew exactly what wanted. The giant mesquite burl that had piqued his interest more than once was now a part of his master plan. It was a huge swirl of gold and black that looked like a boiling cauldron of ore and tar. It had been years since Jacob had payed it any attention, yet now, as it lay in front of him, it seemed to be the perfect final piece to Jacobs puzzle.

He used the saw to cut the smaller trees that grew between the burl and entrance to his mine out of the way. Just as Zicke was dozing off once more, Jacob untied her, loaded the saw and hopped on, in one sudden motion. The ride to the huge knot was a short one, devoid of the typical man-to-mule conversation. It was a small task for Zicke to pull the load to the mine, after Jacob expertly rigged it to her saddle. Dragging it to the mine was the easy part. Setting the trap was another story.

In a fury Jacob began cutting, carving and whittling away pieces of the trees around him. Some were short, some were long and all seemed to have a specific purpose in his mind. It wasn't long before Jacob was sitting in a pile of wood shavings holding each piece of his trap out away from his failing eyes, making sure they were perfect.

After verifying that each piece was perfect, Jacob laid the framework of the trap in the entrance to the mine. Each piece twisted, laid or hung together as though they all were holding each other up. With the rope slung over an oak bush that grew atop the mouth of the mine, Zicke hoisted the key of the trap into its place directly over and in the center of the opening. Jacob traced each piece of the trap with his thick, strong fingers down to the small twig at the bottom that spanned the trail, which entered the mine.

It was the trigger for the trap.

It looked obvious stretching across the bottom of the opening, and as Zicke wandered off, Jacob gathered small twigs and branches in a pile next to his mine. He carefully placed each piece next to the trigger with precision. He couldn't bear the thought of being killed by his own trap. After painstakingly building the perfect replica of a packrats nest, Jacob stood back and admired his work.

The mouth of the tunnel lay wide open to the outside world and Jacob knew that would be a problem. He had seen other miners roll large stones over the mouths of other caves but he did not want to make it too difficult for Riney to find. In a flash of brilliance he came up with an idea.

He dug up four mesquite saplings. He placed each of the saplings in small holes that he dug in front of the mine, leaving just enough room for a man to walk between them. He thought that if there were a decent rain in the next few days the trees would have a chance to survive. But he emptied his canteen evenly amongst all four of the trees anyway. Jacob knew that he had more water stashed on Zicke.

He methodically found the oldest ingredients for adobe lying all around him; dirt and manure. By using only the freshest manure mixed with dirt and most of his water, he made enough adobe to make a small façade for the mine. There were a few out of place branches poking out of the imitation canyon wall. But as Jacob stepped back away from the mesquite trees they seemed to disappear.

The last few drops of water sloshed in his canteen. He slowly poured it all out on the trees, foregoing the quenching comfort of the water for himself and using it all to help ensure the future of his family.

Jacob stepped back and smiled. He looked at the two caches full of ore that lay within a short distance of the mine. He felt proud that he had done more work than he needed too. He had never done the bare minimum and would leave a legacy to his new "son" of doing your best and leaving as much or more than you take. He hoped that Riney would understand.

Suddenly he realized that he was looking at his life's work. He took a moment to let it soak in.

Jacob looked to the east. The sun was very low in the sky and he realized that the day was dwindling. He looked at the four mesquite trees in front of the trap within the entrance one last time and then smiled as he made his way to Zicke.

"Vell, old lady, ve must leave for the last time" Jacob said. "You are much too old for this type of vork und I vould feel bad coming out here on a new, young, strong mule. I vill stick vith my old, broken down, vorn out flea bag." Just then Zicke turned hard away from Jacob and pushed her huge rear end into his chest, knocking him down. Sitting on his own rear end staring at the business end of Zicke put Jacob in a compromising position. But Jacob just smiled when she turned her head back to look at him. He said,

"OK, OK maybe you aren't the only von who is getting older!" Jacob stood up slowly and patted the dust off of his trousers leaving dusty hand prints in a silly pattern across the front of his thighs. He tossed a

piece of candy to Zicke, looked at the pattern on his pants and said, "I look ridiculous."

Jacob loaded his tools into the saddlebags on Zicke. He made his way south, down the mesquite choked canyon, into a huge rocky waterway. He exited into the Salt River Canyon and headed west into the most beautiful sunset he had ever seen.

There were colors in the sky that only belonged to God and magical evenings. The whole sky swirled and changed directly in front of Jacob's old eyes as he rode straight into a beauty that he could never reach. Jacob felt fulfilled, content and tired. He didn't dare blink for a fear of missing even one fraction of it. Quietly he said to Zicke

"Let's go home."

Chapter 13

A Truth

-Everything we hear is an opinion, not a fact. Everything we see is a perspective, not the truth-**Marcus Aurelius**

The rain was falling hard onto each member of the group as they huddled around Paul, awaiting an explanation. The strange question Willis had asked somehow mesmerized everyone else. Paul said two words that shocked me.

"Walt Gassler," came from his lips. He pulled off his backpack that was carrying the fire from the previous stop. Paul continued "was a chef in California in the 1930's. During that time there was a lot of news going around about the mine. Adolph Ruth had just been found, murdered after searching and it made news around the country." Paul had told this story hundreds of times but this time it was different. There was no holding back or changing the information. Paul rubbed his face with both hands and continued.

"Walt had gold fever as bad as anyone, I guess. He wanted to come out here so bad that he got a job at the Biltmore as a pastry chef. He came out a soon as he could. But when he got here he found they had given the job to someone else. That was fine with him because he didn't come out here to make cream puffs. He was here to find the mine."

As Willis continued to stand next to Paul in the rain, the rest of the group found cover. Some sat under trees and some next to large, overhanging rocks but none of them took their eyes off of Paul. They were mesmerized by the story. Paul went on.

"He spent some time at the Quarter Circle U ranch with Tex Barkley and made plenty of notes. There's a pretty famous picture of him standing in front of a huge Saguaro cactus with his walking stick all duded up like he's on Safari. He made a lot of progress back then but not enough. This was the 1930's. The Great Depression was raging, and his wife demanded that he come back and go to work."

"Great story" Steven interrupted sarcastically. "A guy came out here a long time ago and looked for the mine, amazing! You know I wouldn't kick that story down a football field!" The saying was particularly ridiculous and untimely. Still Steven continued, trying to save face, "Not American football, you know like Mexican football? Like soccer? You know," Steven's voice tapered off as he mumbled behind Paul's continuation.

"Walt came back in the 1970's and studied more and more. It's a long story but on May 2nd, 1984 he came back out for one more search. He had asked the two best Dutch hunters to go with him. Tom Kollenborn was a school teacher in Apache Junction and Bob Corbin was the State Attorney General. Neither could go." I watched closely as Leslie pulled the pill bottle from her pack. Her face drained when she found it empty as Paul went on.

"Walt was in his 80's, but he decided to go out alone anyway. Two days later a couple of men found him dead on a rock on Charlebois Ridge." Everyone looked thoroughly confused. This had nothing to do with the Paul's last trip or why Willis wanted to know who was killed. But they hung on each word of the story as it grew even more incredible.

"Tom wound up with some of Walt's things. Just after it happened, a man showed up at Tom's house and said he was Walt's son. He showed Tom a piece of rich gold ore that supposedly came from Walt's pack. The man asked Tom if he could have his father's notes. Of course Tom handed them over." Even though the most exciting part of the story was coming, Paul sounded exhausted. He could hardly talk.

"Later on, another man showed up saying that he was Gassler's son. Tom explained that he had already given Gassler's "real" son the possessions. Then the man proved that he was the real son. No one knows who the first man was but he left with the last gold from the mine and the last clues from the last person to find the mine." Paul paused, rain puddling on his pack, "Walt Gassler," Paul breathed hard as a tear rolled down his cheek, "is the man my brother was named after." He was crying now, "My brother, Willis, is who fell," he said in a broken, shaky voice "and I dropped him."

No one moved. As the rain ran down Paul's face in large, dirty streams they mixed with tears that Paul could not control.

"It's why we came through Le Barge Box instead of up Hoolie Bacon. See that mountain?" Paul pointed at Tortilla Mountain, which was where the other trial lead. It was behind most of the others, who all turned at once.

"That's where I dropped him! That rock, hanging over the edge! I dropped him, I dropped him!" Paul erupted into another uncontrollable sob. The memory was too much to take. Every emotion from that day came rushing back at once.

He could remember how that group had stopped him from going back to the edge to look below. It took two men to hold him down. One of the others had a phone that worked and called 911 right away. The blur of being held against his will and watching the helicopter fly out a black, man sized bag on a rope right past him came rushing back.

No one had the words for the moment. Even Willis just stood in the rain with one hand on Paul's shoulder watching as the man broke down, and understanding why.

After a very unsettling, miniature eternity Paul composed himself. He couldn't look at the clients out of shame for the outburst. His embarrassment turned to confusion when Leslie asked him a question. She was looking straight down at the ground between her feet as she sat on a rock, unaffected by the rain.

"What was the last trip for Paul?" The care and concern that had typically graced her voice was gone. She spoke directly and assuming. She expected the answer to her question.

"It was another search, like this one. I . . ." Paul stopped for a moment. I was curious how he would explain it. He stammered. "We called them "searches". Walt was good at finding folks; he talked to a lot of people on the internet. I talked him into asking the right questions. The questions got people to think that I had found the mine, and together we conned . . ." Paul closed his eyes in a tight squint, "I . . . conned them into paying for the search."

The group began to move, look at each other and sigh or roll their eyes. They knew they were the most recent victims. There was no one who didn't understand. No one that is, except for Leslie.

"Paul you tell me right now that you found the mine between now and then. Don't you tell me that this is another search! You did not lie to us, right?" She had no problem looking at Paul now who could not return the favor.

A thousand lies flooded Paul's mind. Again, he ignored all of them.

"I'm sorry Leslie, this is another search."

Paul did not know how to feel. The overwhelming relief of the truth collided with the fear of it. Paul slowly lifted his head the way an infantryman in a foxhole would at the first sign of a cease-fire. It had been the wrong thing to do. His eyes did not have a chance to meet Leslie's before he was struck in the face by a small, plastic prescription drug bottle. It hit him hard in the cheekbone and landed on the thigh of his soaking-wet pants.

He could tell that it was empty as he caught it in his massive hand. He could see Leslie's name on the label but before he could read the rest she yelled

"It's heroin Paul! Heroin! Don't bother reading the label I'll tell you the truth. That's what they make that stuff out of. Look at me! You at least owe me that!" She pointed to her very flat chest with both hands.

"This is what cancer did to me!" Paul's focus and attention shot to life at the word cancer. He was turned inside-out by the horrible memories of his twelfth birthday. His inner conflict didn't stop Leslie.

"They cut pieces of me off, Paul! They mangled me to try and save my life! And even though they're gone," she moved her hands in circles below her chin, "they hurt! I'm a junkie! I can't spend one hour of my life without those stupid pills. My whole world revolves around pain and pills. There are days I wish I had died, instead of living like this!"

Her motive ripped through the group when she sobbed "This mine was going to pay for my treatment! I spent my last dollar on this trip because you promised me that I would get rich! The gold didn't just represent a better lifestyle for me; it was going to give me my life back!"

Paul had been run through with emotion. He could barely keep himself in his sitting position on the rock. As he searched for something to say or do Willis offered another amazing idea.

"Miss Leslie, maybe I can help. Please come with me." Paul watched Willis slip the money clip into Leslie's backpack, without her knowing. He could hear the gentle older man describing a company in Grand Bay Alabama that would help her. All she had to do was show up.

Paul sat, in silence as the rest of the group thought about what to do with him. Suddenly there was a small outburst from Leslie,

"I can't afford to go to Grand Bay Alabama Willis. I am out of money!" She glared at Paul for the whole sentence.

"Oh, you are a tough cookie, I think that you will find a way Miss Leslie." Willis patted her backpack right on the pocket that now concealed the money clip from view.

"Paul," Taylor interjected, "are you telling us that there's no gold?" As Leslie and Willis returned.

"Guys I have been looking for it for a lifetime. I think I have an idea but it isn't between us and our ride out of here tomorrow." Paul pointed down the trail. "The only thing down that trail is an empty hole and a ride home. If you'll allow me, I'll take you to the canyon where I think it is tomorrow. We have a good shot at..." before he could finish Leslie asked him

"Are you out of your mind? What makes you think that we want to spend another day, on another wild goose chase with you? You aren't the guide anymore, I am. You don't get to come with us tomorrow. I know that we're ending this charade at Tortilla Trailhead. I'm sure you planned on getting a ride out of here with us, so I can't imagine you lied about that. All of the signs say that Tortilla Trailhead is down this trail. We are packing out in the morning, without you!" Her words seemed to deflect the huge raindrops falling heavy on the rest of her face.

"Whoa, now hold on a minute! How am I supposed to get out?" Paul's compassion began to fade.

"I don't care if you don't make it out. As far as I'm concerned you are a missing person who left us in the middle of the night! That's what I'll tell our," Leslie put up finger quotations, "'ride home', if there even is one."

"There's a ride. Leslie, I'm sorry but . . ." Paul stammered.

"No buts, Paul." Davis surprisingly spoke out. "You're out. We are camping further up the trail and you aren't." Davis finished as Steven and Taylor walked closer to him, forming a sort of human wall between the group and their former guide.

"Look you can't keep me from getting to the trailhead. I know these mountains better than . . ." again Paul was interrupted; this time by Jackson.

"Better than what, the inside of a jail cell? Here's the deal Paul, we leave the trailhead without seeing your face and you can be a lost person out here. If you show up at the trailhead tomorrow, you can be a con-man. We control the story Paul, which one do you want us to tell?"

"Guys look here's the truth. I have been looking for a long time. I was going to use the money I made from this trip to find it. Walt Gassler had a journal and I learned some things from it. I think the mine is just over that ridge."

Paul pointed over a small hump on the horizon. The hill had a low spot where the trail visibly went over. "Once we make it to that saddle we turn north. We'll be right on top of it. We can all look together, take even splits and still make it out in time to catch our ride."

"Who's we? You got a mouse in your pocket? We came out here to spend a little time together" Taylor looked at Steven as he finished. "We don't need your money or more of your B.S."

"I didn't even want to mine gold, I'm out." Saffron seemed to be completely undaunted by the affair.

"I don't believe you, I don't need the money, and I already found what I needed out here." Jackson smiled as he spoke.

"I'm sticking with my friends." For the first time on the trip Davis was glad to be on Steven's side, but only for a minute. Steven stepped over to him and hung one arm around his neck as they faced Paul.

"I'm out of pills." Leslie's voice came so quietly that it was hard to hear her. Her complete personality change brought the passion of the conversation down. Then after a short time Willis changed everything, again,

"I," he paused, waiting for everyone to look his way, "forgive you."

No one dared question the sentiment. Willis walked over to Paul, sat down next to him on the rock and finished. "Mr. Paul what you did was wrong. You can't blame these folks for being mad at you. I don't think that you can come out with us. But the Bible and my Mother taught me to forgive always. Not to forgive, unless your guide steals from you, but always. Mr. Paul, I forgive you."

The rain stopped.

Paul could only say thank you in a quiet and humble voice. Then he remembered the fire he had in his pack. The evening was growing colder and he thought that if he could get a fire going it would warm up his antagonists, in more ways than one.

He ripped his pack off of his back and opened the main pouch. The astonishingly dry firewood tumbled onto the wet ground. Paul was excited when he saw how dry it had remained. He reached into the pocket with the tinder bundle and pulled it out. He could smell the smoldering ash from inside. He thought he could win back the group with one more fire.

But he was wrong.

"I'm camping over there." Leslie pointed at a smaller flat spot in the trail about a quarter mile ahead.

"That's fine Leslie, I can build the fire there." Paul began to re-pack the wood into his pack but was stopped short.

"No. I don't need your fire. I know I should forgive you, and maybe I will, but right now I'm leaving and you aren't coming." Leslie slung her pack on one shoulder as she began hiking to the next spot. Slowly each member of the group followed leaving only Paul and Willis. Willis stood up and patted Paul on the back.

"Mr. Paul, you need some time alone tonight." He started to walk away but Paul stopped him with his next sentence.

"I didn't mean to hurt them Willis, or you."

"It wasn't that you meant to hurt us," Willis turned to look back at Paul, "you didn't mean not to." Willis dropped his head in a farewell nod and walked away, easily catching up with everyone else.

Paul's fire looked huge from the other camp. The glow of it lit the canyon into full view all the way around him. He had thrown all the wood that he had carried on it at once. The massive blaze easily chewed through its fuel and grew disproportionate to Paul's needs.

But Paul never moved.

He didn't draw back from its intense heat when it was at its fullest. He didn't boil water, cook food or even scoot closer as it died. He just sat, watching it live and die in front of him.

"Do you really think there'll be a ride for us?" Leslie asked generally to the group as they all watched Paul watch his fire.

"I know there will be. I asked Barbara and Kyle to meet me there. "Saffron had seven yellow flowers behind her left ear. She pulled one out and ate it.

"Barbara and Kyle?" Taylor questioned, forgetting her introduction to the group at Rogers Trough.

"Those are her life-givers, like you are to me. You should pay attention, not Tyler!" Steven said to his father, only this time it was different. This time he smiled and elbowed his dad, playfully.

"Yes, my life-givers," Saffron was oblivious to the sarcasm in Stevens voice. "I didn't know if I could change everyone's mind on the gold. I wasn't sure that a ride home would be on my agenda so I made a back-up plan."

"Good, I don't want to ride home with someone who would be his friend anyway . . ." Jackson said, still glaring over at Paul.

"Hey, don't judge." Saffron drew everyone's attention with her statement. "We all know that what he did was wrong. But we all have done things that were wrong. Maybe not on this level or to this extent but everyone has made a choice that was wrong.

""Wow" Leslie said with a heavy breath out. She was struggling without her medication, "I thought you would be the most upset. You didn't seem to like him."

"I didn't at first." Saffron pulled her hair into a ponytail with both hands, revealing her unkempt armpit hair again. "I don't like what he did but I believe in loving all of nature. Even those of us whose necks are a little redder" she smiled at Taylor, who tipped his hat, "are still nature's creation. I would be a hypocrite if I treated him different because of who he is."

"So what do we do with him?" Davis asked the question that was on everyone's mind.

"Look ya'll, that money I lost coming up here was worth the trip. I think he learned his lesson. I don't want any extra trouble." Taylor said with his eyes closed from under a mesquite tree.

"This thing could've ended at the 'world's biggest juniper tree'" Jackson made finger quotations marks and smiled "and I'd have gotten my money's worth."

"Holding a grudge is like holding a corn dog stick, it don't do you no good!" Steven really thought he had nailed it this time. As the group collectively laughed he decided that he hadn't. Steven stuttered through another attempt "You know, you can dress him up, but, but you can't take him to town." Still nothing.

"So then, what do we do?" Davis asked again.

"Willis are you sure about this treatment thing in Alabama." Leslie seemed to change the subject, though she was not.

"One hundred percent Miss Leslie" Willis's smile was enough to convince her but the words helped as well.

"OK. I guess I could let this one go. It would take me years to get the money back anyway. I won't press charges." Leslie said, unconvinced. Then Willis supported her decision,

"That was the promise you made to him Miss Leslie. Glad to hear that you are a woman of her word."

"So", Leslie continued, as she rubbed her arms to warm them up, "does that mean he gets to keep preying on innocent people? I mean, what's going to happen to him?" She nodded her head towards Paul.

"I think it has already happened." Willis said in his quietly perfect manner.

They all looked back at Paul. He sunk his head into both of his huge hands. No one but me could tell that he was crying. It would be hours before he would go to bed. But the others each found a comfortable spot and fell asleep. Watching Paul had convinced them that they did not need a guard, after all.

The morning crackle of the campfire woke up everyone but Steven, whose open mouth had a small stream of drool running onto his pillow. It was a startling awakening. But even more startling was the person standing next to it.

"What are you doing here?" Leslie mustered up her most stern voice. But halfway through it she yawned, really diminishing the tone.

"Don't worry" Paul said "I'm not trying to follow you out or make amends. I know I screwed up. I figured the least I could do was build you one last fire."

"Paul that's very kind of you." Willis was truly glad. He was the only one.

"No," Jackson said with his back to Paul, packing his bag. "The least you could do is stay in your own camp till we leave, which might have been better."

The silent eternity that followed lasted until each person had packed up camp. No one cared to stay any longer than they had too. They all wanted to be home. With the fire in mid-blaze Willis asked,

"Is everyone ready?" To which everyone but Paul answered yes.

"Then let's pray." Willis grabbed the first two hands on either side of him, Saffron on his right and Davis on his left. As the prayer circle began to form Paul quietly turned and took two small steps away when Saffron said

"Paul, get over here!" It wasn't a kind, laughable command. It was harsh and rude and exactly the perfect thing to say. She dropped Willis' hand and took two steps back. As the circle opened, she reached out for Paul's hand. To the dismay of everyone but herself and Willis, Paul joined. With his head already hung as he entered the circle he grabbed the empty right hand of Willis. The kind old man prayed,

"Our Heavenly Father, as we come to the final day of our journey, we thank you so much for watching over us. We thank you for the lessons we have learned on this trip. Please bless each of us," Willis squeezed Paul's hand, "that we will come away from this trip with a better understanding of life and of the amazing gifts you have given us. Please bless us as we continue on the last leg of the journey that we would be safe. Thank you for all of our many blessings, in Jesus name, Amen."

It was a simple prayer, and a new beginning.

Saffron turned and hugged Paul. Without a word the circle began to revolve towards Paul as each member silently made their peace with Paul. The men shook hands with him but as Leslie approached the tears in Paul's eyes welled up. She didn't know why, but I did.

"I'm so sorry to you Leslie, I had no idea."

"It is not alright Paul" her face melted in forgiveness "but it will be." She managed to give him a hug through much effort. As the company began to make their way towards Tortilla trailhead, Willis stayed back. As soon as they were out of earshot he smiled and said

"I hope you find what you're looking for Mr. Paul"

"I think I will Willis. Just north of that mountain is an old government trail. One of the clues that Jacob Waltz left..." Paul was cut short when Willis looked at him puzzled,

"Oh, you're still thinking about the mine; well I hope you find that too." With that Willis shook hands with a befuddled Paul, slapped him on the shoulder, smiled and walked away.

Paul stayed long enough to safely put out the fire. He followed the same trail that the clients had only he turned off of it once he topped out in a high saddle on the first ridge. Heading straight north he thought about the trip and what all had happened.

He had almost lost touch with reality when he looked up and noticed that Four Peaks Mountain was lined up in a straight line, appearing as one. He turned and looked south and saw Weavers Needle looming large directly in line with the preceding monument. He looked back and forth three times. He trotted to the edge of the ridge ahead of him.

The mesa ran in a north south direction and dropped straight off into a canyon below him. He looked down and saw four mesquite trees growing taller than those around them and very close the wall of the canyon.

Paul scurried down the steep precipice farther down the ridge. He had to re-gain ground by hiking back up the canyon through a wall of mesquite trees. He only stopped when he saw the four giant landmarks he had seen from his perch on the top of the ridge.

As he drew closer to the trees he noticed that they seemed odd and out of place. They were huge and very evenly spaced. They were so close to the wall that it didn't seem possible for a man to fit behind them. Then it happened.

The gust of wind came from nowhere, or so Paul thought. It had magically taken the map that Paul had stolen from Davis and blown it between the two middle trees, just as the map had blown past his face on Tortilla Mountain. As Paul chased it past the huge trunks and up to the wall of the canyon he noticed something that was not really noticeable.

The map had stopped at a small tree limb that was sticking straight out of the wall of the canyon. It was odd because the stick was completely dead and had a carved end. It had been cut by a blade and placed in the wall of the canyon.

Paul looked very closely at it. He put the map in his pack without looking away. He recently had a hunch about this canyon but right now his hunch felt stronger than ever. He grabbed the branch and pulled. With little effort from the huge man the stick came out. With it came a piece of the wall about the size of a soccer ball.

Paul started pulling away at the small fissure and found the whole wall to be a type of adobe. There were all types of wood within the entrance. Paul felt as though he had stumbled on the fountain of youth.

His pace quickened and before too long Paul was staring into an open cavern, filled with debris of every size and shape. In the bottom of the entrance was, what appeared to be a packrats nest of small twigs and branches. He noticed a huge knot from a mesquite tree hanging above his head, and right in front of him. It was beautiful piece of wood that looked like a pot of boiling mesquite. As he stepped closer to get a better look at the oddity he heard a small twig break.

He didn't have time to look down. All he could see was the ornate interlacing of the deep gold and black grains in the wood as they grew closer and closer to his forehead. Then, there was nothing.

Chapter 14

The End

*-Every new beginning comes from some other beginning's end-**Seneca***

The particle of dust floated in on a hot gust of wind. Its path through the long, slender window at the top of the room was ironic. The window had been designed to let the warm air out of the building, not in.

It floated casually past the books on the top shelf where millions of other particles had come to rest. They lived on the tops of books that no one had checked out in years. It slowly and indirectly swayed downward past the other book shelves. The orange colored light in the room made the speck almost invisible as it came into the vicinity of the librarian.

She looked like a librarian. She wore a hand-knitted shawl draped around her neck, though it wasn't cold. Her black, horn-rimmed glasses sat at the tip of her nose, though she wasn't reading. It was the uniform of a librarian and she wore it proudly, though at this moment she didn't care much about her uniform.

She was asleep.

The particle rose and fell with the breath exiting and entering her mouth in huge, silent waves. With each surge the particle got closer and closer to her gaping jaw until, in a sudden snort, it was consumed into her right nostril.

Her own obnoxious sneeze woke her suddenly.

As she gathered her senses and daintily wiped any evidence of the sneeze from her nose, mouth and surrounding book covers, she looked around the library. It seemed empty. She was relieved that she had not been caught sleeping, snoring or sneezing by any students. After all it was after normal school hours and typically there weren't many students that cared to spend more time than necessary with her.

But today wasn't typical.

Today, behind one of the huge, overstuffed shelves, in the back corner of the room sat a boy. She recognized him but had trouble remembering his name. As she glanced around she saw that they were the only two there. He seemed completely absorbed with his reading.

She was elated that he hadn't been too terribly distracted by the outburst. She felt certain that he had heard her but he did not care. He was definitely not studying. Kids looked for every rabbit trail in the library to consume their attention rather than the study at hand. This boy was here on his own, studying something that engulfed him in a way that an English assignment could not.

He was on a treasure hunt.

She rose from her chair and walked slowly to him, trying to give herself enough time to think of his name. She took half steps and quieted her feet giving herself time to think, so that she could spurt out his name as she walked to the table. But she arrived no more informed than when she started.

"What's got you?" she asked, not really sure how to approach him. Recognizing his face as he looked up but drawing a complete blank she looked quickly at the mess of books and old newspapers on the table in front of him. All she saw for certain was that one paper was opened to the obituaries.

"Oh the same as usual, the Lost Dutchman's gold mine." The boy smiled as he answered, and his answer jogged her memory.

"Pauline" she said, relieved at the memory," if any adult knows more about that mine than you I'd be surprised. What did you learn today?" She tried to make it her business when a student took free time to read. She tried to re-enforce the effort if she could.

She was a good librarian.

"Well I know a lot about the mine already. I'm trying to learn about the people. You read a lot about their lives but I'm trying to find out what happened to them." Wanderlust shone in Pauline's eyes as they darted to one of the yellowed newspapers.

"What do you mean?" She knew exactly what he meant but wanted to keep his enthusiasm going. It was contagious and she enjoyed it.

"Well, like this one" Pauline pointed to a very small blurb under a picture of a man. The picture itself looked sad. It was an old photo of a man from the collar up. The black and white tones were so disproportionate that only the upper right side of the man's face was lit. The rest of him was dark. He looked thin and was old. The shape of his bald head matched the downward turn of his mouth. His eyebrows were turned up slightly in the middle of his forehead, apologetically. He stared in a combination of sorrow and guilt. Above the stricken figure was the scribbled cursive name: Rheinhart Petrash.

"This is Riney. He spent his whole life looking for the mine and never found it. The Dutchman gave him all the clues and waypoints to the mine when he was young. He was like a stepson to Julia Thomas. It says here that he committed suicide in Globe." Pauline dumped facts in his excitement without explaining much of the context. The word suicide gave the librarian shivers. She changed the subject rapidly with a question.

"Who is Julia Thomas?"

"Oh you don't know about Julia?" Pauline could hardly wait to move onto a different key figure. The librarian hoped that this one had a better end.

"Julia was a mulatto"

"Pauline that's not nice." The interruption surprised Pauline. He really didn't know what the word meant. But he had read the word in so many of the descriptions of her that he previously thought it meant a woman who sold ice cream. But now he thought that it must mean gold-digger.

"Well she was one. The Dutchman showed up when she needed him the most. Her husband left her and she owed $2000 in bills for her ice cream shop. It says here that 'All of the debts were paid with ore matching the ore used by the Dutchman on various occasions'."

"So" she asked "was Julia his girlfriend?"

"It doesn't say anywhere. He spent the last years of his life around her and Riney. He gave all the clues to them after he was too old to keep mining." At that the room erupted with yet another sneeze. Another particle of dust had triggered the shocking sneeze once again.

"Bless you." Pauline looked truly concerned for her well-being. Remembering the first sneeze he asked "You aren't getting sick are you?"

"Heavens no, it's just allergies. Please go on."

"OK," Pauline continued, "it gets kind of strange here. Some writers say that she loved the old man and cared for him in his last days. Others say she was just a mulatto."

"Pauline, stop it!" She interceded.

"OK, a gold digger," she was confused as Pauline continued, "who just waited for him to die so that she could get the gold herself. One book says that she was selling tickets outside his room while he was dying. People bought 'em so that they could ask questions about the mine. I think that maybe she was his closest friend after Weiss."

Who in the world is that?" She glanced at a clock. There were still a few more minutes until she could close up. She decided to spend them with Pauline.

"Well that whole story gets a little tricky too. The Dutchman had a best friend. See here is a book," he scrambled through the books and papers and pulled out an old hardback. It was laying face down and open, "that says his name was Weisner, with an *n*. Then, this one" he closed the first book and set it aside without giving his student enough time to see what the book was.

He grabbed another one and thumbed through it. As he did she could distinctly read the name of the author. It was Sims Ely. But before she could make out the title on the worn out cover he opened to a page. "See here they call him Weiser. This is the story of how he died." She again felt a certain discomfort about the subject but her curiosity got the best of her.

"What does it say?"

Pauline began to read.

"Apaches jumped me, I knew they'd killed my partner first. Apaches got all the animals 'cept one horse. I rode him a few miles, but the goin was slow, and then their arrows stopped him. I got one in the arm, but I kept goin. Runnin', then stoppin' behind rocks to fire my rifle at 'em. They were afraid to come close, and at last they turned back. I made for the first water hole on the desert I knew about."

"He did an interview before he died?"

"No. See the doctor that found him, Dr. John Walker took care of him while he was dying. When he realized he was going to die he gave Walker the map to the mine."

"Oh, so Dr. Walker found it then?"

"No, it gets even juicier. Dr. Walker already had lots of money. He had a mine called the Vekol. He left the Dutchman's mine alone. He wound up giving it to his friend, a man named Tom Weedin. Before Weedin could go look for the mine, his wife burned the map. She was worried that he would die like everyone else who looked for it. So the real map is gone forever." Pauline looked sad until the librarian asked.

"So why do you call him Weiss?"

"Oh, right here," Paul sifted through some copies of old, official looking papers, "a purchase record of the Grose Lode claim in 1864." She was blown away with the veracity of the young man's research. "J.C. Weiss bought a mine from William Grose on January 5th. I wish we knew his real name but I always imagine that this," Paul thumped the paper, "was his best friend. This seems like the kind of guy who would brave Mexican robbers with the Dutchman to go get the map from Peralta."

"Peralta?" She looked at the clock. There was still time and her interest was growing with every word that came from Pauline's mouth. For a young man he was very influential.

"Ooh" Pauline began shuffling newspapers around. "Don Miguel Peralta was who had the mine first. Well maybe not first but he had it before this was America." Pauline was looking straight down as he rifled through page after page of an old yellow newspaper.

The name on the top of the front page was hidden as it had folded over on itself. But suddenly Pauline slapped it down on top of a small stack of books. "He was the guy that the map came from in the first place. I read that he had a gambling problem and came back and forth from Mexico to here when he was old. Then I found this." Pauline lifted his hand, which was rather large for his age, off the paper and revealed a small article.

In bold print on the top were the words 'IN NOGALES' stamped out in all capital, block letters. Under it were two columns. The one on the left had a beautiful cursive script reading "The Oasis" under which was typed the date. Saturday, Nov. 6th, 1897. The right side had the description that seemed to have Paul mesmerized. It read

Having some business yesterday morning at the room of Mr. Miguel Peralta, who had been the bookkeeper at his store, Mr. A.F. Paredes went to the room of the gentleman, on International street, and was shocked and horrified to find him stretched in death upon the floor; a bullet wound in his head and a pistol in his hand with a discharged cartridge told that the fatal wound had been self inflicted. The authorities were notified, and Justice Duffy impaneled a coroner's jury who took the testimony of several who knew of some facts bearing upon the case. Mr. Thomas Harrison testified that about three o'clock in the morning he took the deceased (who had been drinking and gambling) to his room. Mr. E. J. Pellagrin, in the adjoining room, heard the shot, but thought it a piece of furniture falling. Mr. S. D. Piper, who lives in the vicinity also heard the shot. The two witnesses agreed that the time was between three and four o'clock. Mr. Paredes introduced a note from the deceased which was found on the table with a Mexican dollar resting upon it which read; "I had the money; I have lost it: good bye."

Pauline could tell that she was done reading, but didn't know what to say. She looked up slowly from the paper and asked,

"Do any of these stories have a happy ending?"

"Well it's been so long that all of them are dead. But I guess the Dutchman was the last happy story about the mine." Pauline didn't have to look at any of the papers or books to tell this story. It all came from his head.

"He lived to be 81. He would've lived longer but in 1891 the Salt River flooded. His property was right on the river and he got stuck in the flood. The rescuers took him to Julia's house and he stayed sick for a while. It seems like everyone in town knew the Dutchman was about to die." Pauline started to look through one of the books but then he remembered whatever it was he thought he had to look up.

"Dick Holmes and other snakes waited around his bed, hoping he would die so they could rummage around and dig up some of his treasure. The flood was in February but he didn't die until October. They say that Julia didn't even go to his funeral. Dick Holmes took 50 pounds of ore out from under his bed while he was still in it. He told everyone it was a gift. They say he went straight away and started digging up the old man's property."

"That doesn't sound like a very good story Pauline" the librarian wrinkled her eyebrows.

"Don't you see? It is a great story because he did have a mine! He found it, mined it and didn't die trying. He won! People like Dick Holmes, Herman and Riney Petrasch and Walt Gassler spent their whole lives looking. He spent his doing."

"Pauline" she looked straight into his eyes "sometimes the search is what's important, not the finding."

Pauline had no answer. He looked down at the stack of literature in front of him. To him it was more than just a mountain of information.

It was a pile of lives. He turned his head back to the kind librarian. She smiled and said,

"Chop chop, we should've been gone five minutes ago."

Pauline looked up at the clock and his eyes widened.

"Whoa! I didn't know it was this late!"

He put his books back into place as fast as he could as the librarian helped with the newspapers. He grabbed his small steel lunch box and said

"Thanks for the talk Mrs. . . . ."

Before he could finish she responded.

"No Pauline, thank you. Why are you in such a hurry anyway? Got a date?"

She smiled and raised her eyebrows

"Well it is a big day for me. Daddy is home from the mine for the first time in forever! I can't believe he got today off. Usually he is working."

"Oh? Is there something special about today?" She prodded.

"Well, sorta." Pauline offered up his best awe shucks look as he swayed back and forth.

"Well are you going to tell me, or is it a mystery like the mine?" She smiled.

Pauline could no longer contain his excitement or his smile. He bubbled with happiness as he answered

"Today is my birthday! And this year were having my favorite, a huge German chocolate cake! Momma promised me last night. It's gonna be great!"

"Well happy birthday Pauline. Who knows, maybe today you found the missing piece to the puzzle to the Lost Dutchman! Maybe you'll find it someday because of something that you learned on your, hey how old are you anyway?"

Pauline beamed as he answered

"Twelve."

"Well, have a great twelfth birthday. Now hurry up and go get some of that cake!"

"Bye Mrs." Before he could finish, she interrupted him again.

"Good bye, Pauline."

Chapter 15

A Beginning

-To know that we know what we know, and that we do not know what we do not know, that is true knowledge- **Confucius**

Paul flinched. He threw his hand up in the air to protect himself from the falling burl. His eyes closed tightly as he waited for the crushing blow to land on his head. He looked so silly standing outside the mine, flinching from nothing that I almost laughed.

After standing in the utterly ridiculous pose for much too long, he slowly relaxed. He stood up straight and looked around. As I expected, he looked confused. He wasn't sure why or even how he was standing outside the entrance to the mine. That he was confused was a good sign. It was a confusing situation.

He walked around in circles for a moment trying to make sense of it all. He reached up and touched his head. There was no lump or pain. He felt for his backpack but it was gone. He spun around quickly as if to look at his own back where the pack had been. Of course that was futile. No one can see their own back.

Even in his state.

He sat on a medium sized rock that lay against another, enormous boulder. Each had been a part of the cliff above him at one time. But their time at the top had ended in a crashing slide to the bottom of the canyon. He looked up to where the rocks had once been and noticed an eagle on a tree.

It was so far up that the bird looked tiny. There was evidence of the destructive path that had carried the boulders from the eagle's position to where he was now. As in all things, change had taken place.

Paul took the moment to try and make sense of what was going on. The last few days had been like nothing he had ever experienced before in his life. This search had been like no other, and it was about to get even stranger.

Sound exploded above his head and was so violent that he fell off the rock. It was massive amounts of air being displaced and sounded like it was right on top of him, though he didn't feel anything when it happened.

He heard the turmoil in the sage next to his sitting rock. As he quietly peered through the bush he saw the massive golden eagle on the other side. It was the bird from the top of the ridge. She was so close now that Paul could see her dark black talons digging into the small rabbit she had captured.

As she repositioned herself on top of her meal, Paul noticed that she was half as tall as he was. He looked back at the rock where he had been seated. It was only a few feet from the bird. Then he looked to the tree where he first noticed her. He was confused. He didn't understand how the bird had missed him. As she dove for her prey she had to have passed just above the rock where he was seated.

He quietly adjusted himself to a more comfortable position, watching the bird as it pecked the hide off the now dead rabbit. He had never been this close before. Most eagles would fly off if Paul was within thirty yards of them. Now here he sat, less than six feet away.

It was a sight that most people never see.

As he made slight adjustments, he knew each small movement could alert the bird to his presence. But with each small motion the eagle never looked. Paul moved again, this time faster, and still no reaction from the bird. Suddenly behind Paul a rattlesnake let out a buzz from its tail. The bird looked towards the sound and stared straight at Paul. He froze. It reminded me of the Bacon and Upton tank and the story in the rain, about the last search, when Paul looked straight at me.

The bird waited cautiously for the whirring to stop. When it did, she went right back to her meal with no concern for Paul, which concerned Paul. He stood up quickly, no reaction. He waved his arms, no reaction. He jumped up and down, I reacted. I could no longer hold it in. He looked so silly that I belly laughed uncontrollably.

He heard.

Paul spun quickly in place gazing straight at me. Tears welled up in his eyes. He had cried more in the last few days than he had since he was twelve, but this one was different. This time the sob came ripping from deep inside of him. He could hardly see from the huge tears pouring from his eyes and streaming through the stubble on his face. Through his uncontrollable breathing he finally said my name.

"Walt?"

I was ecstatic. For the first time in the trip he could see me. I had been worried that he wouldn't recognize me because I knew I was different now. I had hoped that I wouldn't have to convince him of who I was. Fortunately I didn't.

"Hello Paul," I finally got to say.

Confusion, anger, sorrow, pity and love all twisted his face into a heap of loss. He was stricken for words, answers and questions. I could see the realizations hit him one at a time. I was dead. But I was here. That means I wasn't gone. He just couldn't see me if he was alive and I was dead. But he could see me now. That meant . . .

Paul turned to face the opening of the mine. His view was blocked by one of the huge trees that Jacob had planted so long ago. Paul took three huge steps to his left to see beyond the tree and before he could take the fourth he stopped.

Between the two massive trees in the middle was a dark opening in the cliff. It had been befuddled by old adobe, branches and sticks that Paul remembered tossing out of the way. Towards the middle of the opening lay an enormous ball of mesquite that almost filled half mouth of the cave. It was dark black with bright golden swirls of grain.

Paul recognized it immediately.

As he looked closer he noticed, at the bottom of the opening, under the large knot were two boots. The placement of the boots seemed symbolic. The bottoms were pointed towards us. Most of the boots lay inside the shade of the tunnel. But the two souls were outside the cave, which was hilarious to me. Paul was not laughing as he realized that they were his boots.

"I'm dead," Paul speculated. "I mean, we're dead. Walt I'm so sorry. I'm sorry I dropped you. I tried my best, you have to believe me. The straps broke," he was getting mildly hysterical now "I couldn't do anything." Paul paused for a moment as his clarity grew with his rambling. He paced as he talked.

"I guess I didn't have to bring you out here. I didn't have to start this whole mess. Maybe there was something that I could do, or something that I shouldn't have done. Walt I never wanted you to get hurt. I was just trying to make us a living. I didn't think that it would lead to this. I never thought it would kill us."

"It's killed a lot of people before." The words sprang forth from my mouth. It wasn't something I would normally say to Paul. It seemed I had little control of when I could talk and what I could say.

"I know. I thought we, well, I thought that I was different "Paul's speech quieted. "I thought that I would find it and that we would be set for life."

"Well, you found it." I almost felt bad about that sentence, but I couldn't stop what I was saying.

"Yeah, and look what it cost me. I guess I was wrong about a lot of things wasn't I? I was wrong about what finding the mine would do to us, wrong about the searches," Paul stopped pacing and slowed his speech. "I was even wrong about the afterlife."

"You were right about where the mine was." For some reason I could not allow him to talk of the afterlife with me. That was a conversation for someone else.

"Well, yeah. That's why I looked, so I could find it. Now that I've found it I've lost everything. I spent my whole life, just looking, and what did I ever get from looking?" Paul was talking himself through a lot. "I mean, I guess I learned a lot. I didn't really know that a guy like Willis could be, well, a guy like Willis."

"Of course there's Saffron." I said thinking of her eating the flower from her hair.

I smiled. Paul did not.

"How do you know about . . ." Paul stopped . . . "You've been with us! Walt, you were with us, weren't you?"

I could finally tell him.

"Yes. Paul, when you were telling the story of my fall to the group you looked right at me. At the tank when you were talking about friends it was like you were talking to me. Paul, the loud boom at Rogers Trough that you all argued about," I couldn't say anything else. I wanted to, but when I tried to speak my mouth stayed closed. It was out of my control.

"That was you?" Paul realized that the noise he heard was me entering. I could speak again,

"That was me. I have been on this whole trip brother. There was a lot that happened to you, and around you. Some you noticed, some you didn't. This search was special."

"What did I miss? What happened that I didn't see?" Paul asked with the curiosity that had been lost since we were kids.

I tried to open my mouth to tell him about the conversation that Willis had with Jackson about the tree. Paul had missed that entire exchange. I wanted to explain to him how the group all decided to let him escape the clutches of the law, even though what he had done was despicable. I thought of the way that Steven and Taylor were feeling towards each other, or the change in Saffron's thinking or how Davis felt about having friends. I wanted him to know that Leslie would be OK. I wanted to explain the whole thing to him. But I couldn't. Again my mouth would not open.

"Walt, what did I miss? You must've seen everything. Please tell me."

I wanted to. But I couldn't even tell him that I wanted to. Something was stopping me. Then we heard a voice from behind Paul. It was a man's voice that boomed loud off the walls of the canyon. Even though it seemed to echo to us, the eagle continued to devour her rabbit.

"Don't you sink zat he vants too? Vy don't you shtop und use your head for more zan just a hat stand."

Paul wheeled wildly around and faced his antagonist. He was a plump, large man with a white beard that flowed to his belly. He stood very close to Paul and, though he was a bit smaller he made a very imposing figure. He was completely in Paul's space, forcing him to take a step back as soon as he turned. The man chewed on his own lip, causing his beard and mustache to wiggle in separate directions.

"Are you," Paul stuttered "I mean you have to be. You're him! You're, you're Jacob Waltz!"

"Of course I am. Who else vould be here, shpeaking zis vay und looking as I do. I can't believe zat zis is how you sink of me. Fat und old. You sink I vas really zis fat, und zat my accent vas zis bad?"

Paul looked confused. I was confused. Then, as the eagle left the carcass of the rabbit and flew back to her perch on the top of the cliff, Paul realized a piece of the puzzle, and taught it to me.

"So I am seeing you guys the way I think about you, the way I remember you?" He looked into Jacob's face for an answer.

"Are you asking?"

"No, well maybe. This is all new to me. I don't really know."

"Of course you know. Maybe you don't have confidence but you know zee answer. Zere is a huge difference between knowing somezing und having confidence in it. You knew zee mine vas here und you had zee confidence to come und find it. Even zoe you are very shtupid, you found it because you had zee confidence."

"OK so I am seeing you as I think of you, not as you are. It makes sense that you have changed and I wouldn't recognize you now. So, Walt doesn't really look the same and you don't really have the accent, or the belly."

"Now you are getting zee hang of zis."

"So, why won't you answer my questions?" Paul said out of frustration.

"Paul you have certain rules that you have to live by. Laws of science, motion and nature right?" I could finally start to understand the times I couldn't speak.

"Well yeah, of course, gravity is a law I guess. It was the law that killed you. But now," Paul looked down at our feet. He noticed that mine and Jacobs were not on the ground. I could see the revelation hit him.

"You live by a different set of rules than we do. Well no, I mean we have a different set of rules because I'm dead too right?" He looked down at his own feet. They were planted firmly in the dirt.

"So I'm not dead, or I am? What is going on? Tell me what is happening. I can see myself over there," Paul shot his thumb over his shoulder in the direction of the mine, "dead. How come you are floating and I'm not? Is it because I'm not dead? Maybe I am dead and you aren't. What is happening?" Paul screamed his question.

"Paul, think of some of the questions you asked me." I was beginning to understand clearly. Jacob smiled at my progression.

"I asked you what is going on. I asked you what I missed on the search. I asked you if you had been with us the whole time and if the thunder was you." Paul's memory was surprisingly good.

"Okay . . ." I was unable to tell him about some of the questions he had forgotten like if he were dead and why he was still standing.

"Of those questions which ones did I answer?"

"Well, you said you were with us for the whole trip and that the thunder was you. But I already had those things figured out. Those questions weren't really questions just . . ." then it hit him.

"You can't tell me anything I don't already know!" The next sentence slowly dripped out of Paul's mouth. "That would take away my faith."

"Vell, look who decided to use his brain! You know zat it took Adolph Ruth only two quvestions to figure zat out? You have a long way to go my friend."

"You met Adolph Ruth?" Paul asked, and then promptly answered his own question. "Well, of course you did. He's dead and you're dead and you couldn't tell me if I didn't already know. So you met Adolph Ruth." Paul stated the sentence this time, rather than asking it.

"But I never believed in this," Paul waved his arms around. "Life after death! I know better than that, so how can you be here talking to me if I don't believe this is even true."

"Paul what was the last thing you did before you left the group?" I realized that I could ask him questions that led him to the truths that he didn't already know, without telling him the outright truth.

"I said goodbye."

"You really are shtupid! Before zat." Jacob was growing tired of Paul. Apparently Paul had always thought Waltz was a very impatient man.

"Well, I prayed with them." Suddenly a rush of information filled my head and I was able to share so many things.

"Right Paul, you prayed. That is proof that you believe something. You're silly pride has made you like so many others. They try to outthink their heart and rationalize some outrageous belief that there isn't an afterlife. They think that there can be nothing bigger than them or that they are in control. Then, in a split second when things are at their worst, almost all of them do something completely out of character. They prey. They might say the silliest prayer like 'God, if you're out there' or 'OK, if I do this then you'd better do that' but they all believe. They have all believed their whole life just like you." I could see tears welling up in his eyes. "But like Jacob said, there is a difference in knowing something and having confidence in it. You have always known you just didn't have confidence."

"I hurt a lot of people Walt."

My uncontrollable answers continued, "You sure did. But. . ."

I wanted to tell him about the letters he would receive from each member of the last search. That Taylor would explain how much better his relationship with Steven was, how Davis had started to meet people and even went out on a few dates.

Saffron would write from somewhere in New Mexico that she had met a man named Edison who introduced himself as 'the best looking Indian to ever ride a horse.' She thought of Paul. She would write him explaining how she and Edison would be life-givers.

Jackson would send an email from his new startup, Tate Academy. It would go on to make him two times as much money as he had in real estate working half the hours. He was now friends with Pat Flynn, the man that Davis had mentioned to him.

But the best letter would come from Willis. He would explain that Leslie had undergone the new experimental treatment that his company had engineered and was not only better, but she was representing the company as a spokeswoman. Willis would explain that none of it would have happened without the search. In typical Willis fashion, he eluded to something that Paul would never understand how he knew. He would write,

"Glad you found what you were looking for," just above his signature.

I wanted to tell him all of these things that would come, but I couldn't. Jacob looked at me sternly as if he knew what I was thinking. I understood my own limitations now. Instead I told Paul,

"Mom loves you." The words shocked me even though I said them. Paul broke down once again. When he gained his composure I said, "But, I couldn't say it, if you didn't already know."

Paul rose to his hands and knees from under the huge mesquite burl. The pounding in his head caused him to swing it back and forth slowly, as if he could move it away from the source of the pain. A small trickle of blood ran down his forehead and dropped onto the ground between his hands. He reached up and touched the stream. It was running down a swath of dried blood that had poured out of his head as he lay under the log. Paul could barely stand.

Slowly he made his way outside the mine. He found the two boulders that looked so familiar and sat on the smaller of the two. He reached for his pack and found that it was there on his back. It was a strange case of differing déjà vu. He had done this all before but with a different outcome. Then it all rushed to him.

The memory of what had happened hit him all at once. He looked to where he had been standing and saw no footprints. He looked back to the mine and saw no boots. He took a drink from his canteen and slowly turned his head to the eagles perch high above him. There was no eagle. Then he turned his head to the brush just a few short feet away from the rock.

Lying behind the bush, within arm's reach of Paul was the carcass of a freshly killed and eaten rabbit. There were tufts of hair and tracks in the sand, all around it. Paul leaned towards it, causing his head to throb even more. But as he looked closer he could see the scratching on the ground of a huge bird of prey. The marks were so large it could only have been an eagle. Even though there was no way to know what type from the marks on the ground, Paul knew it had been a golden eagle.

Paul sat up. His head hurt but he was getting accustomed to the pain. It wasn't going away; he was just coping with it. He poured a small amount of water into his hand and gingerly rubbed the dried blood off of his forehead. He sat back and rested his upper body on the larger of the two rocks as if in a rocking chair. He thought about what had happened.

Then he remembered where he was.

In the blink of an eye the pain left his head as he stood up and turned around. As he glared between the trees he realized that he had been lying in the entrance to the Lost Dutchman's gold mine! He had found it! The feeling was like nothing he had ever felt before.

Paul had spent his entire life actively waiting for this one instant. It was surreal as he stood facing the subject of his dreams. He looked around and imagined Jacob Waltz working the mine over a century ago. He had imagined it thousands of times but this time he imagined a much thinner man.

He thought about the riches that awaited him inside. Paul only needed to walk in and become a millionaire. He thought about how his life would change. Then, in a flash of clarity, he thought about how his life had already changed.

He had spent the last part of the search caring for the clients and it had felt good. He learned that there was more to a man than how he appears. Willis taught him that. He watched a small woman face unbelievable adversity in the form of cancer, addiction and weather. He saw Saffron change her mind. He understood that he had grown every time he searched for the mine.

He didn't want to take that away from anyone else.

He knew that if he finished what Jacob Waltz started that the news would spread like a brush fire, and the Lost Dutchman would no longer be lost. Paul thought about all of the people who would come with stars in their eyes. Hope and trials would teach them some of the same lessons he had learned. He understood that finding the Lost Dutchman would be like telling a child not to imagine. He could not take the wonder and awe of this from someone else.

He rolled the huge mesquite burl into the mine, opting not to re-set the trap. Paul did the best he could to close up the entrance. It felt so strange that he was not only leaving it, but covering it up. He placed some of the large branches in a criss-cross pattern over the gaping hole. He filled in the small openings with mud made from the dirt around him and a puddle left in the river bed nearby. He stepped backwards from the Lost Dutchman's gold mine two steps and stared. He wiped a trickle of blood from his forehead and smiled. He finally understood that the best part of this place was not in the finding, but in the searching.

Paul sat back down on the rocks and prepared for his short hike out to Tortilla Flat. He rested his injured head against the larger rock behind him and braced with his right hand. As he adjusted his weight he felt something strange in the rock. There was an odd indentation, almost hidden from view. As he bent to look closer he saw names etched into the rock. Most were names he recognized, some were not.

Each name was carved at a different depth and in a different style. Paul realized that each name on the list were people who had been here before! He read closely the names of Adolph Ruth, Walt Gassler, Tom Kollenborn and Bob Corbin to name a few. These were all men who Paul knew were Dutch hunters. They were infamous in the lore and legend of the mine. He had always wondered why none of them were able to seal the deal on the Lost Dutchman.

Now he understood.

Paul spent an hour scratching his name on the backside of the rock. He was leaving his mark amongst others who had learned that the search is more valuable than the finding. After he left, I walked over to the list and smiled at the perfect lettering of the final name on the list of greats.

It read:

PAULINE MICHEALS.

Bibliography:

The Bible on the Lost Dutchman Gold Mine and Jacob Waltz. By Helen Corbin

Senner's Gold. By Helen Corbin

Quest for the Dutchman's Gold. By Robert Sikorsky

The Sterling Legend. By Estee Conatser

Superstition Mountain A Ride Through Time. By James Swanson and Tom Kollenborn

Hikers Guide to the Superstition Wilderness: With History and Legends of Arizona's Lost Dutchman's Gold Mine. By Elizabeth Stewart and Jack C. Carlson

The Lost Dutchman Mine of Jacob Waltz. By T. E. Glover

When Silver was King. By Jack San Felice

The Story of Superstition Mountain and the Lost Dutchman Gold Mine. By Robert Joseph Allen

Recipe for The Search:

2 cups of Jim Rohn

2 cups of Andy Andrews

½ a cup of Malcolm Gladwell

3 tablespoons of Seth Godin

1 tablespoon of Patrick F. Mcmanus

Add Pat Flynn, Andy Stanley and Dave Ramsey to taste.

Preheat the mind of John Henderson to A.D.H.D., combine all ingredients and half-bake for years.

You can find more about John at johnhenderson.org

John Henderson

Made in the USA
Coppell, TX
22 August 2023